DAN EMMETT
WITH CHARLES MAYNARD

★ ★ ★ ★ ★ ★ ★

I AM A SECRET SERVICE AGENT

My Life Spent
Protecting the
President

ST. MARTIN'S GRIFFIN

NEW YORK

I AM A SECRET SERVICE AGENT. Copyright © 2017 by Dan Emmett. All rights reserved. Printed in the United States of America. For information, address St. Martin's Press, 175 Fifth Avenue, New York, N.Y. 10010.

www.stmartins.com

The Library of Congress Cataloging-in-Publication Data is available upon request.

ISBN 978-1-250-13030-3 (hardcover)
ISBN 978-1-250-13031-0 (e-book)

Our books may be purchased in bulk for promotional, educational, or business use. Please contact your local bookseller or the Macmillan Corporate and Premium Sales Department at 1-800-221-7945, extension 5442, or by e-mail at MacmillanSpecialMarkets@macmillan.com.

First Edition: June 2017

10 9 8 7 6 5 4 3 2 1

For the men and women of
the United States military, Secret Service,
and Central Intelligence Agency.
And, for the young men and women
who will one day serve our nation
in these tremendous organizations.

★

Contents

Contents

★ x ★

★

The Man in the Arena

It is not the critic who counts; not the man who points out how the strong man stumbles, or where the doer of deeds could have done them better. The credit belongs to the man who is actually in the arena, whose face is marred by dust and sweat and blood; who strives valiantly; who errs, who comes short again and again, because there is no effort without error and shortcoming; but who does actually strive to do the deeds; who knows great enthusiasms, the great devotions; who spends himself in a worthy cause; who at the best knows in the end the triumph of high achievement, and who at the worst, if he fails, at least fails while daring greatly, so that his place shall never be with those cold and timid souls who neither know victory nor defeat.

—President Theodore Roosevelt

★ ★ ★ ★ ★ ★ ★ ★

I AM A SECRET SERVICE AGENT

*

Introduction

Secret Service agents are expendable when it comes to protecting the president of the United States. All Secret Service agents live with the knowledge their lives can be exchanged at any time for that of the president. That thought is always present in the back of an agent's mind. In every Secret Service agent's career, there are moments that bring this reality home. These times remind agents that their lives are not their own, but belong to the United States of America and the office of the presidency.

Many times during my career, I was reminded of this fact. On one occasion my assignment was to prepost in a room where President Bill Clinton was to meet with Syrian president Hafez al-Assad. To prepost is to be in the room before the president arrives in order to scout and prepare for anything. I was not there to cover and evacuate the president in an attack. My purpose was to neutralize any threat to the president of the United States (POTUS).

This meant I might have to kill the Syrian bodyguards if they drew their weapons. I suppose I should have been flattered to be chosen for this assignment. I realized that if I did have to shoot the Syrians, like them, I would in all likelihood be experiencing the last day of my life.

Before entering the room, I took a few seconds to think of my wife and family. I said a quick prayer to the effect that if called upon to kill the Syrians, I would do it quickly and accurately, and President Clinton would live even if I did not. As my prayer ended, I was filled with a calm rage. I decided that no matter what, I would do my job to the best of my abilities. True to my training as a marine, I would accomplish the mission at all costs. Suddenly it was game time.

My orders were to enter the conference room before the president. When presidents Clinton and Assad came in with their security details, I made eye contact with the Secret Service shift leader. In the exchange of looks I understood that the Secret Service controlled the room, not the Syrian bodyguards.

I slowly moved behind Assad's men to gain the best firing position. I saw from the outlines through their tight-fitting jackets they carried Skorpion machine pistols. I understood the Skorpion well from terrorist weapons training. I knew how to fire one and what it was able to do. Since the Skorpion was a short-barreled .32-caliber, fully automatic weapon, it was not very accurate. This meant that in a small space, shots could go anywhere. This could endanger the president's life. That could not be allowed.

As I stood behind the Syrians, I began playing the "what if" game, running battle scenarios. If the Syrians drew their Skorpions, my training taught me to shoot each threat twice with my Sig Sauer pistol. I was to fire until 1) there was no longer any danger; 2) I had no more ammunition; or 3) I was out of the game.

I moved to a better position, so President Clinton and Assad would not be in my line of fire in case I had to shoot. I did not want to accidentally hit the very person I was to protect. It would be terrible if a Secret Service bullet from my pistol struck either POTUS or Assad.

Thankfully the Syrians never drew their Skorpions and I did not have to kill them, nor they me. However, the incident was a cold reminder of what Secret

Service agents are expected to do throughout their careers.

Who are the men and women that protect the president of the United States? Where does America find such people who are willing to face danger and to sacrifice themselves for the office of the presidency? How does the search for men and women determine which are worthy of trust and confidence?

WORTHY OF TRUST AND CONFIDENCE

Almost every organization has a motto. For the Boy Scouts it is "Be Prepared." The Marine Corp's motto is "*Semper Fidelis,*" or "Always Faithful." "Fidelity, Bravery, and Integrity" is the FBI motto. For the United States Secret Service, the motto is "Worthy of Trust and Confidence."

All Secret Service agents carry a small wallet-like notebook known as the "Commission Book." In the Commission Book are a badge, a photo ID, and a statement of the agent's authority under federal law. The law states that agents can Carry Firearms, Make Arrests for Offenses Against the United States, and Provide Protection for the president of the United States. The Commission Book also states that the bearer is Worthy of Trust and Confidence. This means citizens of the United States of America can trust the Secret Service agent in all matters of national security.

Sometimes people think Secret Service agents are cold-blooded, steely-eyed bodyguards with large biceps and dark glasses. For the most part, agents are like everyone else. Agents are fathers, mothers, sons, and daughters. They are your neighbors, friends, relatives, coaches, PTA members, and fellow citizens.

Yet in other ways, they are very different. The main difference lies in what each is prepared to do. The men and women who are worthy of trust and confidence are willing to lay down their lives without hesitation for the office of the presidency. Their training ensures their ability and willingness to give their life without question. This primary mission of keeping the president alive at all costs sets the Secret Service apart from other government agencies.

My career was not unique. This book could be about any Secret Service agent who served on a presidential detail. Since 1902, thousands of agents have been worthy of trust and confidence and prepared to protect the president with their lives. This is my own story of working within arm's length of the president of the United States.

★ 1 ★

The Death of a President and the Birth of a Career

I served as a special agent in the United States Secret Service from May 16, 1983, until May 16, 2004. While a special agent, I had the honor and deep responsibility to protect three sitting presidents. Through my years of being a special agent, I learned there is no such thing as a routine day. Anything and everything was possible. On any given day, my work could go from a morning run with the president, to the boredom of answering phones in the office, to the thrill of flying on Air Force One. Some days I did all three!

Many people ask how I chose the Secret Service

as a career. The answer is complex. The main part of my answer is that children are very impressionable. When I was only eight years old, the murder of President John F. Kennedy changed my life.

Over that fateful November weekend in 1963, I decided I wanted to become a Secret Service agent in order to protect the president of the United States. Twenty years later, that is exactly what I became. Through hard work and a little bit of good fortune, my dream grew into reality.

BEGINNINGS

I was born in the small town of Gainesville, Georgia (about fifty miles northeast of Atlanta), the third of three sons. My parents worked hard to provide a good life for my brothers and me. They carefully planned everything. My brothers and I were each six years apart so that no two of us were in the same school at the same time. None of us were in college together. In my parents' lives nothing seemed to happen by chance. Planning was one of the most important lessons I learned from them. Always plan ahead! And, have a back-up plan and a backup for the backup. I often heard my dad remind my brothers and me, "Prior planning prevents piss-poor performance." I found this good advice, as with most things he said.

My parents worked to make sure their three sons graduated from college. Even though my parents went to high school but did not go to college, they made sacrifices to make sure that their sons did.

My parents were born after World War I and grew up during the Great Depression. Both of their families had little money in their early years. But through hard work and good planning, they accomplished many amazing things during their fifty-nine years of marriage.

My dad was a serious, self-made man who did not seem to have much of a childhood. The son of a cotton mill worker who also served as a Baptist minister, Dad dropped out of high school at sixteen to work in the mill and helped support his family of two brothers and four sisters.

My father fought in the Pacific during World War II. After the war, he remained very patriotic. He joined the American Legion and the Veterans of Foreign Wars. Dad loved God first, his family second, and baseball third . . . although the order could vary depending on what teams were in the World Series.

After my parents married, Dad found he had a talent for business. He quit his job as a mill worker, and became a furniture salesman. Within ten years, Dad started his own furniture business, the Emmett Furniture Company. He owned this business for sixteen years before moving on to other endeavors.

My mother was the picture-perfect mom of the late 1950s and early 1960s. Always well dressed, she cleaned our house and did other housework clothed like TV moms on popular shows. It did not matter how busy she was, she always seemed to have dinner on the table promptly at six o'clock when my father arrived home from work.

Growing up, I got to spend a lot of time at Dad's furniture store. We always called it "The Store." Most days during the school year, Dad sent one of his two deliverymen (Robert or Reeves) to pick me up from school. They drove me to The Store where I did my homework, played in the large area of the rug department, or watched the newest black-and-white TVs. One of my favorite things at The Store was the drink machine. For a dime, usually given to me by Dad from the cash register, I got the coldest glass-bottled Coke in the world!

The smell of new furniture and fresh floor wax filled the old 1920s building. Interesting people came and went all the time. Police officers, local politicians, businessmen, just about anyone you could think of and a few you would not have thought of came through The Store. Dad was a friend of Congressman Phil Landrum from our Ninth Congressional District. One day while I was watching cartoons in the TV section of The Store, Congressman Landrum came in. I felt very special when this important man who worked in the nation's capital sat and talked with me for a few minutes.

Some days after school Robert or Reeves would drop me off at the public library where my mother worked part-time. At the library, when I finished my homework, I devoured books about World War II, the military, or guns. My mom's coworkers, who considered me "cute," fussed over me. Often they gave me dinner-spoiling treats and delighted in patting me on my blond, crew-cut head.

I attended Enota Elementary School within the Gainesville City School System. I got a great education in a school system that over the years produced many doctors, lawyers, and engineers. Also, two astronauts and a couple of Secret Service agents came from those schools.

Each day following morning Bible readings, the Lord's Prayer, and the Pledge of Allegiance, we studied reading, writing, arithmetic, and American history. At recess, we played hard, always to win.

Sometimes our enthusiasm resulted in bloody noses, scrapes, cuts, and bruises.

In addition to regular fire drills, our school also prepared for a nuclear attack. My parents and grandparents had practiced bomb-raid drills during World War II. By the time I was in elementary school, my classmates and I listened carefully to what we were to do in case of a nuclear attack by the Soviets.

We practiced evacuation drills. Since there was no good defense in the case of a nuclear attack, the idea was to send everyone home in order to be with their families. Traveling the great circle route, an Intercontinental Ballistic Missile (ICBM) took about twenty minutes to launch from the Soviet Union and reach the United States. I remember one time when given the signal, all students got into groups, and we all walked home.

In the fall of my second grade year, these evacuation drills took on a new urgency. The Soviet Union shipped nuclear weapons to Cuba just ninety miles from the United States. I later learned this was called the Cuban Missile Crisis. All I can remember is that my teachers and parents talked about things in hushed tones and seemed to be worried.

President John F. Kennedy appeared on TV to talk about these Soviet missiles one evening. Kennedy was the youngest person ever elected to be president of the United States. I liked him. I knew he was very important by the way my parents talked and watched him intently. This crisis passed, and school life continued.

At "show and tell," my friends and I brought all kinds of things for our classmates to see. We tried to outdo each other and bring really interesting objects. Once, a buddy of mine brought a fully automatic .30-caliber M2 carbine that his father, a police captain, provided. Guns played a large role in my upbringing. At a young age, my dad taught me how to use a gun, including all the safety rules. He told me, "Never point a weapon at anything you do not intend to kill or destroy."

When I was eight, I roamed our neighborhood with other gunslingers, my faithful Daisy BB gun in hand. Often, several boys in our neighborhood wandered around with their BB guns. Sometimes we carried actual firearms, usually a .22 rifle. Other than not having as many birds around, we caused no damage and no one was ever hurt. No one ever lost an eye or was rushed to the hospital.

We tried to get the most out of our BB guns by shooting things at the utmost limits of the gun's range. By trial and error, I learned the basics of shooting, including how to adjust the rifle's sights to account for wind and elevation. These experiences became valuable later in my life after I joined the marines. Firing an M16 rifle or an M1911 pistol came easily due to my early self-training.

Many of my relatives served in the military in World War II and Korea. Dad's World War II service included helping liberate the Philippines from the Japanese. Like many World War II veterans, he spoke little of his military career. During the rare times he did talk about the war, I listened carefully, completely fascinated by his exploits.

My Uncle Olan, an army tank platoon commander, fought in North Africa against the Germans led by Field Marshal Rommel. During one battle, the Germans captured my uncle. He spent the rest of the war in a Prisoner of War (POW) camp in eastern Germany. Uncle Olan suffered as a POW. He nearly froze and starved to death several times. He came home with a medical discharge, a broken man. My uncles Fletcher and Bud fought in Europe and barely survived their experiences.

The sons of these men, the next generation, also served their country in the armed forces. One of my cousins became an officer in the air force and flew combat missions in an F-4E Phantom over Hanoi in

Vietnam. Another of my cousins became a naval officer aboard a nuclear attack submarine. Still another of my cousins lived in Germany married to an army infantry officer.

Growing up around military veterans, I always understood my duty was to serve America. I felt it was my destiny, just as it had been for my father, cousins, and uncles. Most of my relatives simply assumed I would contribute in the same way with military service. It surprised no one in my family when I became a Marine Corps officer. But my service to the United States would turn out to be a great deal more than military service.

A DEFINING MOMENT

Friday, November 22, 1963, began just like any other day in the third grade. I left school that afternoon glad the weekend was beginning. As I walked down the sidewalk, someone said that President Kennedy had been shot and was dead. I figured it was a hoax, because something like that could never happen.

The green "Emmett Furniture" pickup truck pulled up at the school. Robert, Dad's deliveryman, picked me up that afternoon to take me to the store for the usual afternoon of homework and playtime.

I struggled into the cab under the weight of my military pack filled with textbooks. Inside the truck, Robert was wearing his usual aviator sunglasses and smoking his usual Phillies cheroot.

Normally Robert was quiet and reserved. He seemed disturbed about something.

"What's wrong, Robert?" I asked.

With difficulty he answered, "President Kennedy's been assassinated."

Puzzled I said, "What does 'assassinated' mean?"

Robert swallowed. "It means the president has been killed."

"You mean the president is dead?"

While looking straight ahead, he simply and quietly said, "Yes."

The world changed in that moment. Without my realizing it, so did my life.

The five-minute trip from the school to the store seemed to last much longer. We rode in silence listening to the news on the radio. When we got to The Store, many of Dad's customers stood in stunned silence watching the news on three or four televisions in the TV Department. The newsman told the details of the assassination that had happened in Dallas, Texas.

No one seemed to notice me. Dad's customers talked quietly about Russian or Cuban involvement. They may not have thought I understood any of it. The Russian part worried me. I remembered from the year before when we had to practice going home due to a possible nuclear attack during the Cuban Missile Crisis. According to those gathered around the TVs, if the Russians had killed the president, there would certainly be war.

Over the weekend, I watched live TV as President Kennedy's coffin arrived at Andrews Air Force Base (AAFB) near Washington, DC, in Maryland. I would come to know Andrews well twenty-seven years later. I remember seeing the president's blood still on First Lady Jacqueline Kennedy's legs and dress as she stayed with the former president's coffin. I also recall the new president, Lyndon B. Johnson's, first address to the nation. I did not like him. He was completely different from John F. Kennedy, whom I liked a great deal.

Later, on Sunday, November 24th, my family and I watched as the accused presidential assassin, Lee Harvey Oswald, was gunned down on live TV. He was in the Dallas police headquarters. Since I did not yet know about due process and guilt beyond a reasonable doubt, I remember feeling that justice had been done. The man everyone seemed to believe had killed the president was also dead.

Up until that point, I—along with everyone else in America—was in shock over the assassination. I could not believe John F. Kennedy was no longer president. I did not remember Dwight D. Eisenhower as president. It seemed Kennedy had been president my whole life. Now he was gone. As depressing as the entire situation was, a moment was about to occur that would change my life forever.

In the middle of all the confusing and emotional events of that weekend, I saw a picture taken moments after the fatal shot to Kennedy. The photo showed Secret Service agent Clint Hill on the back of the presidential limousine. Agent Hill had jumped onto the car at the sound of the shots to protect the president and Mrs. Kennedy by shielding them with his own body.

When I saw the picture, I asked my father, "Who is that man?"

"He is a Secret Service agent," replied Dad.

"What is he doing?"

"He was trying to block the assassin's bullets with his body."

I could not quite understand the idea that a man's

job was to place himself in front of a bullet meant for the president. At eight years of age I didn't understand everything, but I knew enough to understand that being a Secret Service agent sounded very important . . . and very dangerous.

In that one picture I could see Agent Hill's unquestionable courage and devotion to the president. I also saw the importance of the Secret Service. Without a doubt, that one picture inspired me to become a Secret Service agent. Children are indeed impressionable. President Kennedy's death and the picture of the Secret Service agent on the car changed my life. I wanted to be *worthy of trust and confidence* and to live within arm's length of the president of the United States. I wanted to be a Secret Service agent.

Preparing to Serve the Country

As the years slipped from one to the next, so did my ideas of what my career would become. I wanted to be everything from an astronaut to a surgeon. In the end, two career ideas always returned. I continued to want to be a commissioned military officer and a Secret Service agent. I saw the military as my patriotic duty and a place where I could exercise my healthy spirit of adventure.

Even as a child, I took risks. I enjoyed quests. I liked things just dangerous enough to produce some adrenaline. Many afternoons I rode my homemade skateboard down our street as fast as possible with no helmet or protective pads. As I grew older, the machines became more dangerous, and my love for them became more intense. That love was dampened a little on a summer day in 1971 when I crashed my Mustang Mach I into a tree. Two weeks later the car was repaired, and I continued on my way, excited to be in control of a 351-cubic-inch V8 engine. However, I drove with slightly more care.

When I graduated from high school in 1973, I enrolled at North Georgia College, a military college only twenty miles from my hometown. I chose this college for its academic excellence and for its ability to prepare me to serve my country. All males living on campus were required to be in the Reserve Officers Training Corps (ROTC). This meant that I wore a uniform and learned the customs of the US Army.

North Georgia College's commandant of cadets had graduated from West Point and served in the Korean War. He was one of the finest men I have ever known. As the fighting in Vietnam began to wind down while I was in college, the army started to change. The army moved from a conscript force to an all-volunteer army. Recruiting commercials invited young men and women to "Join the People Who Join the Army" and offered, "Today's Army Wants to Join You."

I began noticing marine recruiting commercials and posters that boasted of keeping its standards high and its ranks small. "We're looking for a few good men," declared the marines. The hard-nosed Marine Corps approach intrigued me. However, I had never met a marine officer. No marines worked at North Georgia College.

I learned that the marines came to our campus to find good candidates for their officer programs. Once a quarter, the marines set up a booth in the student center for one or two days. Students dropped by and talked to the recruiters about opportunities in the marines. Interested students took the Marine Corps officer's written exam. One day I decided to see what the marines had to offer. Captain Kenneth L. Christy led that recruiting team.

On a beautiful autumn afternoon, I drove to a motel near campus to take the exam. I first met Captain Christy when I pulled into the parking lot. He had just gotten out of his car and was walking across the pavement. He looked the part of a military officer. A little over six feet tall with large biceps, he was a slightly smaller version of one of my favorite TV cowboy actors.

He exhibited a large chest created by thousands of bench press repetitions and a small waist honed from thousands of miles of running combined with hundreds of thousands of sit-ups. Captain Christy looked more like a model wearing a marine uniform than an actual marine. In addition to his imposing physique, he wore aviator-style glasses and sported extremely short hair.

His perfectly tailored uniform was completed with silver parachute wings and three rows of combat ribbons. He had been awarded the Bronze Star and two Purple Hearts from his 1967 tour in Vietnam. His highest award, the Bronze Star, had a combat *V* for valor. Years later, at no request of his own, the Bronze Star was upgraded to the Navy Cross, the nation's second highest award for valor, only after the Congressional Medal of Honor.

After introductions, Captain Christy invited me into the motel lobby. We sat down to talk about the marines and my interests. I had come to take the marine officers' exam. However, it soon became apparent that Captain Christy was actually interviewing me to see if I would be allowed the *chance* to take the written exam!

Sizing me up, Captain Christy hinted that from the looks of me, I probably could not make it through marine training. He suggested I might think about another branch of military service. I could not tell whether he was serious about my appearance, or if he was trying to offer a challenge designed to attract someone seeking a challenge. Either way, I was sold on the marines!

Captain Christy suppressed a smile and summoned his equally impressive gunnery sergeant. He directed the sergeant to give me the officers' written exam. If I passed, my journey into the armed military service of the United States would begin. I would start with the Marine Corps Platoon Leaders Class (PLC) program.

The PLC program trains college students as officer candidates during the summer at Marine Corps Base Quantico, in Virginia. After receiving a degree, a successful candidate was awarded a commission as a second lieutenant in the US Marine Corps. It sounded easy to me, but I would learn differently.

I sat down at a small desk. The gunnery sergeant handed me the test booklet for marine officers. Four long hours later I finished the test . . . and passed! The next step would be to attend the Marine Corps Officer's Candidate School (OCS) Platoon Leaders Class program. As a teen, I was undisciplined and rebelled against authority in all forms. Now, I had somehow chosen the most disciplined branch of the military service.

I knew I needed the type of discipline only the marines offered. As the great football coach, Vince Lombardi, once said, "There is something in all good men that yearns for discipline." I apparently yearned for discipline also. I would soon learn it under the most trying conditions.

As the day for OCS drew nearer, the reality became sobering. It was one thing to pass a written exam, but quite another to go to the training, or even to get on the plane to go. I thought about a line from a movie when an actor said, "How can I lead other men? I don't even know where I am going." That pretty well summed up my leadership skills at the time.

HELL UNDER THE VIRGINIA SUN

Marine Corps Platoon Leaders Class is no summer camp! PLC is physically and psychologically brutal! It is designed to produce officers who will lead the US Marine Corps. This was a crucial time in my life. During this training I became the person who would be a marine officer and a Secret Service agent.

From the minute I arrived in Quantico, every waking moment was a challenge to survive. On most days, my platoon mates and I would have bet that none of us would live through the summer, much less graduate.

Over the next weeks, we ran five miles every morning wearing leather combat boots that seemed to eat the skin off our feet. Even with shaved heads, the constant, humid Virginia heat cooked our brains. During all this, the staff physically and verbally harassed us. I had been around profanity on summer construction jobs in high school when I worked with ex-cons, including a few convicted murderers. None of these guys held a candle to the Marine Corps Drill Instructors (DIs). The DIs took profanity to a level approaching art. Their ability to weave meaningful profanity into every sentence spoken was almost awe-inspiring.

Each day brought new difficulties. Every Saturday morning after three hours of physical training, we stood motionless on an asphalt parade deck for inspection. The oppressive summer sun beat down on us, cooking us alive. Candidate after candidate collapsed from heat exhaustion. The staff did practically anything short of killing a candidate to determine the candidate's fitness to be a Marine Corps officer.

The days began at 0430 (4:30 a.m.) with physical training that had killed strong men, hospitalized many, and caused others to quit. The long days ended with lights out at 2100 (9:00 p.m.) when we fell into bed and slept like the dead until it all started over again at 0430.

One DI, Staff Sergeant McLean, was twenty-eight years old, six feet five inches tall, and carried no unnecessary body fat. With piercing blue eyes and a booming voice that could be heard for miles, he was the Hollywood poster image of what a Marine DI should look like. Staff Sergeant McLean, a veteran of Vietnam and one of the last marines to leave, served as a DI at Parris Island. There he trained enlisted marines.

I knew from the first moment I saw him that I could expect the best and most severe training allowable under the Uniform Code of Military Justice. He did not disappoint. As our primary tormentor, Staff Sergeant McLean threatened every day that if we did not straighten out (he used more colorful language) he would personally kill us or, even worse, send us home before graduation.

Another DI, Gunnery Sergeant Gilpin, who shaved his entire head every morning, repeatedly informed us, "If you actually believe YOU are going to serve as officers in MY Marine Corps, you are crazier than shit-house rats!" He said this to the entire platoon sometimes and at other times to an individual. None of us had any idea what a shit-house rat was but we figured it must be in some way worse than the standard rat.

Gunny Gilpin was a master of head games and played them at the strangest times. One morning before physical training (PT), I was seated in the head—the bathroom—with my red USMC shorts at my ankles. The Gunny came in and sat down on the toilet next to mine. In those days there were no partitions separating the porcelain thrones. No one else was in the head. There were twenty other choices. The Gunny chose to conduct his business right next to me! Comfortably seated and reading the newspaper, the Gunny carried on normal small talk with me as if we were old friends. I started to catch on that our DIs were decent guys who were actually human beings. However, ten minutes later on the PT field, the Gunny became the inhumane maniac we all loved and admired.

The training at Quantico consisted of Marine Corps history, drill, weapons, leadership, and tactics. These subjects, combined with never-ending physical training, occurred under the critical gaze of battle-hardened officers and enlisted DIs. These men always searched us for leadership potential. The Marine Corps believes that before one can lead and give orders, he must first learn to *follow* orders. Failure to immediately carry out orders to the letter meant punishment for the candidate. This form of training worked.

One punishment required a man to run the quarter-mile around the asphalt parade deck while holding an M14 rifle (10.32 pounds) above his head. If no rifle was available, a footlocker was used. He did this until he either collapsed in the summer heat, or the DI thought he had learned his lesson.

These punishments could be given for something as small as not remembering one of ten general orders, having a dirty rifle, or anything the DI felt important. DIs thought *everything* was important. The point was to teach instant obedience and attention to detail. Everything was designed to save lives in combat. The training program tested who could think and function well when pushed to their limits. The question was, "How badly do you want to become a Marine Corps officer?"

Every other week we went on twenty-mile forced marches. Each man carried only two quarts of water and a rifle while wearing full field packs and a helmet. The sun beat down on us during 95-degree summer days with 100 percent humidity. The DIs pushed, dragged, and yelled at those who fell behind. The verbal abuse was unimaginable. Many dropped due to

I Am a Secret Service Agent

heat exhaustion, heat cramps, or heat stroke. These men were put in a large truck with a navy corpsman who shoved in an anal thermometer and then packed them in ice. I thought death would be better than this humiliating life-saving measure. If a man fell too far back, the DIs put him in a safety vehicle and he disappeared from the training, never to return.

One of the most important lessons we learned—Never Quit! Never quit even when you feel you cannot make it any longer. Never quit even when you think you cannot take another step. Never Quit, because quitting was not an option in the real world of combat.

Once during a three-mile run, a platoon mate threw up. Throwing up on a difficult run was not unusual. It happened. However, the DIs did not like my friend stepping out of formation and stopping to get rid of his morning chow. When we got back to the platoon area, we showered and dressed for the rest of the day's training. While standing at attention in front of our racks (beds), we noticed that one man was missing: my friend who had stopped to throw up. About that time, the old screen door of our 1942 Quonset hut flew open. A host of DIs propelled our buddy into the center of the squad bay. We hardly recognized him! Brown mud covered him from head to toe. He got that way from having to crawl through various mud pits and culverts around the base. This demeaning treatment taught us that if a marine quits in combat, much worse things could happen. From that day forward we learned to throw up while running.

We also learned the art of fighting with a bayonet. Each man had an M14 rifle with bayonet attached. Staff Sergeant McLean taught us the basic moves of the thrust, smash, slash, and horizontal rifle butt stroke. We studied how best to place cold steel in an enemy's guts, to smash his face, and to beat his head into pulp. We practiced these moves hour after hour. We worked until the ten-pound rifle felt like it weighed *twenty* pounds. Over and over we repeated each movement until we could fight without think-ing. Then it was time to practice on each other—with pugil sticks.

A pugil stick is the size and weight of a rifle. It looks like a giant Q-tip with padding on both ends. Each man dons a football helmet and groin cup and is paired with an opponent. At the DI's whistle, each man does his best to deliver what will be a lethal blow or at least knock his opponent down with his "rifle." About two seconds into the match, all the moves we learned and practiced went out the window. Each man simply used his pugil stick as a club to pound on his opponent.

The exercise instilled fighting spirit and aggressiveness, as well as teaching bayonet fighting. Like modern-day gladiators, the men fought one another under the DIs' watchful gaze. The DIs often bet on the outcomes. If a man did not appear to be aggressive enough, he fought TWO others. This continued until he could no longer hold his weapon or seemed to possess the sufficient killer spirit to be a marine officer.

In order to teach merciless killing, a match was not over until the DI blew his whistle. Even if a man was on the ground, the victor continued to pound the vanquished until the whistle sounded. This was literally the school of hard knocks!

I fought in two bouts. In the first, I soundly beat my opponent. However, in the second, I woke up staring at the clouds in the blue Virginia sky through the grill of my football helmet. In baseball, batting .500 is great! In bayonet fighting, .500 is not considered very good. The biggest lesson I learned that day was before I engaged a man with a bayonet, first I would have to be out of ammunition.

Nearly half of the candidates left the program. The merciless, extremely hard training was designed to convince as many candidates as possible to Drop on Request (DOR), to Quit! The idea was that if a man would quit on a run or a march, he would probably quit in combat. This type of man needed to be identified and weeded out.

While many from other platoons quit, none from my platoon dropped out. Nor did anyone from the ten platoons run by Staff Sergeant McLean during his four years as an OCS DI. Up until that time no other DI had matched that record. In addition to that record, no other candidate or DI bested our DI's three-mile run time of less than seventeen minutes.

As hard as OCS training was, quitting never entered my mind. Of all the things I learned about myself that hot Virginia summer, Never Quit was perhaps the greatest. That lesson would later serve me well as a Secret Service agent. When challenges tested my nerves and stamina, my mind and body, I succeeded by never quitting.

As the days and weeks slowly passed, the DIs never let up their relentless pressure. They constantly reminded us that being dropped from training, even on the last day with our families sitting in the graduation stands, was always possible. There was method to this madness of the DIs. They knew that those who graduated would be Marine Corps officers.

They knew that one day we might command them. Each DI wanted to be certain we were competent to lead them under the worst conditions. They went to great lengths to make sure we were up to the task.

With each passing day, as the training became more vicious and the ranks dwindled, one thing was clear: It did not matter what we were doing—twenty-mile forced march, a five-mile run, bayonet training—Staff Sergeant McLean, the other DIs, and the officers always participated. They led from the front. No one ever commanded us to do anything they could not or would not do themselves. Leadership by Example was hammered into our very souls during that hellish summer under the hot Virginia sun. I took that lesson with me throughout life and to the Secret Service.

The night before graduation, I sat on the cool cement floor in our dark squad bay. Three of my best friends and I drank vodka and grape Kool-Aid from a metal canteen cup stamped "1944" on the bottom. I kept that cup, which now sits on my desk, as a reminder of the lessons I leaned that summer.

On graduation day the ordeal finally ended. The survivors stood on the same parade deck where we had endured so much misery. We hardly believed we had made it. We began with over 600 candidates and finished with 321. Final class rankings were based on three areas: physical fitness, academics, and leadership. I came in 118th. While my final ranking was not superior, even the man who finished last at 321 had much to be proud of.

At the graduation ceremony, Staff Sergeant McLean shook hands with me and smiled one of the few smiles I ever saw on his face. He congratulated me on finally getting myself straightened out. I have never forgotten that day.

Marine Corps Officer's Candidate School gave me my first experience in a world where a man was expected to do his job and do it well. No awards came our way. Graduation was the reward. Doing one's job was simply expected. With the hell of OCS now behind, I headed back to air-conditioning, cold beer, civilization, and the rest of college.

The September after OCS training, I was shocked with the news of an attempt on President Gerald Ford's life. Fortunately, the gun did not fire, and the Secret Service agents (among others) acted quickly. The Secret Service quickly moved President Ford out of harm's way. Only two weeks later another assassination attempt occurred. This time shots were fired. I saw the replays on the news that evening. Secret Service agents put themselves around the president, shielding him with their bodies. They pushed President Ford into the limousine and rushed him away. With the summer's training, I was more than willing to be a Secret Service agent, but that had to wait for the right time.

I graduated college with a degree in criminal justice. Later that summer, I realized the long-sought-after goal of being commissioned a second lieutenant in the US Marine Corps. As I stood at attention in my summer service alpha uniform, I took the oath of a commissioned officer. I scarcely could believe it. The whole day was a blur. I had worked for so many years to reach this seemingly impossible goal. I felt it was all happening to someone else while I was just watching.

I celebrated through the night and into the next morning. When I awoke sometime around noon, I saw my uniform scattered about. It dawned on me that I was now a Marine Corps officer and no longer a civilian. It was a great feeling that helped lessen the hangover.

My first assignments were to Basic School and

the Infantry Officer Course. I moved on to the Second Battalion, Ninth Marine Regiment at Camp Pendleton, California, where I proudly served for four years. I commanded from 38 to 180 enlisted marines. I used all the traits and leadership skills taught by my DIs and officers at OCS.

As a leader, I continued to progress. I had learned above all else that the most important thing was to lead by example. If a man leads from the front, others will follow. In years to come, this leadership tactic would be critical as a Secret Service agent. Eventually, I would train new agents and lead other agents while protecting the president of the United States.

ANOTHER DEFINING MOMENT

Even though I enjoyed my marine service, I decided to leave active duty when my expiration of service rolled around in November 1981. My decision had become clear on March 30, 1981. I had just come in from a five-mile run with my marines.

"Lieutenant Emmett, you should listen to this. The president has been shot, sir."

Only the sound of the radio filled the company office. The announcer said that President Ronald

Reagan had been shot in Washington, DC, outside the Washington Hilton.

I immediately thought back to that November afternoon in the third grade when Robert told me about President John Kennedy's assassination. I remembered my confusion and how quiet the adults in The Store were, how they stood around the TVs. It all came back to me.

I jerked back into the present. All the marines in the company office quickly moved to a TV to hear more news. Video of the assassination attempt ran on every network. We watched the shooting over and over, even in slow motion. We saw President Reagan waving to a group gathered outside the hotel, when suddenly six shots were fired. It all happened so quickly, it was hard to understand until it was run in slow motion. The Secret Service agents of the Presidential Protection Division (PPD) reacted immediately at the first shot. Special Agent in Charge Jerry Parr shoved the president into the limousine. Secret Service agent Timothy McCarthy, using his body as a shield, jumped between the shooter and President Reagan.

As I watched all this, I remembered the picture from John Kennedy's assassination when I was a child.

Seeing Secret Service agents place their lives on the line to protect the president had awakened my desire to become an agent.

In the days that followed the shooting, we learned President Reagan had been wounded along with three others, including Secret Service agent McCarthy. Also, I understood why Special Agent in Charge Parr's quick thinking and actions had saved the president's life.

With the attempt on President Reagan's life, and my military service coming to a close, I focused once again on my never-forgotten childhood dream— to be a Secret Service agent. Although I did not have any idea how to do it, I started to try. After all, I was a marine officer. Even after I hung up my uniform and grew my hair to a normal length, I would always be a marine officer. I looked for a way to achieve my goal, and I would not quit. I would not give up.

★ 3 ★

Never Quit Unless You Are Dead

Once I was discharged from the marines, I immediately began the quest to become a special agent with the United States Secret Service (USSS). This turned out to be much harder than I thought. For months, no one in the Atlanta field office of the Secret Service would return my calls. I was calling the Atlanta office, because all agent applications are handled through the field office closest to the applicant's home. Since I lived in Gainesville, Georgia, Atlanta became my recruitment office.

I spent most days working out, helping teach scuba, and taking flying lessons. I took a job in a local bank just to keep from going broke. The next year, on a slow summer day, I called the Atlanta field office for the fifth time in as many months.

"United States Secret Service. Atlanta Field Office."

My heart skipped a beat. "May I please speak with an agent?"

"What is this in reference to?"

I had learned that if I said I was interested in applying for a position in the Secret Service, the call would be over. So I said, "I can only speak with a special agent."

The receptionist hesitated but connected me to the duty agent.

"How may I help you?"

"I would like to apply to be an agent in the Secret Service."

"I am sorry, but the agency is not currently hiring agents at this time," he said hurriedly. "And not at any time in the near future."

Rather than saying, "Thank you for your time, sir." I continued to keep the agent on the phone with questions about the Secret Service. He finally gave up on getting me off the phone and promised to send me an application. I would not take no for an answer. This was too important to me. The Marine Corps taught me that if an objective cannot be taken one way, find another. Never quit, unless you are dead.

When the application arrived, I completed it immediately, sent it in, and then waited. Several weeks later the office manager called to inform me that the special agent in charge (SAIC) wanted to interview me for an agent's position. My persistence had paid off. I got an interview. Now it was up to me to make the most of this rare opportunity very few ever got.

I drove excitedly to Atlanta for an interview with Special Agent in Charge Jerry Kivett. As I sat in the waiting room, I realized this was one of the most important days of my life. I had to make the most of it.

I was nervous as I entered SAIC Kivett's office. Jerry Kivett was something of a Secret Service legend. He had served on the detail protecting Vice President Lyndon B. Johnson on November 22, 1963, when President Kennedy was assassinated. Kivett stood watch on Air Force One when Johnson took the oath of office to become president of the United States.

Trying to appear calm and confident, I firmly shook Agent Kivett's hand. I wanted to make a good impression on this man who held my future with the Secret Service in his control. Mr. Kivett wasted no time. He came directly to the point.

"So, Dan, why do you want to become a Secret Service agent?"

I took a deep breath. "Since I was in the third grade when President Kennedy was assassinated, I have wanted to protect the president," I started. I then talked about the picture of Clint Hill on the president's limo in Dallas. I don't really remember all I said after that.

Kivett stared at me in silence for what seemed a long time. "Have you seen the video of the shooting of President Reagan?"

"Yes, sir."

"Did you see the Secret Service agent protecting him?"

"Yes, sir."

"Do you think you could do what that agent did when he placed himself in the path of the bullet meant for President Reagan?"

I thought for a moment and then said, "The Secret Service must have a great training program. From my experience in the marines, I believe that I respond well to training. I hope I never have to be in the position of the agent who was shot. But I am confident I would respond according to training."

Mr. Kivett smiled slightly and said, "That is a very good answer."

There I sat before a man who had been in President Kennedy's motorcade in Dallas on November 22, 1963. This was a man who had been under fire during the assassination of a president. This man knew better than most what being a Secret Service agent really meant.

My "good answer" allowed me to advance to Round Two. Agent Kivett sent me next door to the assistant special agent in charge (ASAIC) of the Atlanta field office, Robert Coates. "Are you looking for a job?" Agent Coates asked me.

"No, sir," I replied. "I am looking for a career in federal law enforcement."

Agent Coates asked more questions about my background, training, and experience. He wanted to know about my time as a marine officer. He even inquired what I knew about the Secret Service. Finally, the interviews ended and I drove the fifty miles home. I had given my best answers. I hoped they were good enough.

I continued my boring bank job. A few weeks later, the office manager in the Atlanta field office called again. Agent Kivett had selected me to take the written exam for special agents in the Secret Service. The test, known as the Treasury Enforcement Agent Exam, was hard, very hard. It tested vocabulary, reading comprehension skills, observation skills, and ability to do complicated math word problems.

I took the test with four other applicants. I passed! In fact, I was the only one to pass. I scored 73 out of 100. For the first time, I was optimistic about becoming a Secret Service agent.

Months passed with no word from the Atlanta office. Then one day, with no warning, I was requested to appear back in Atlanta for a panel interview. This phase of the selection process was one of the last major hurdles to becoming a Secret Service agent. The panel consisted of three senior agents who for hours asked a long series of questions.

Agent Robert Coates, now the special agent in charge after Agent Kivett's recent retirement, introduced me to the other members of the panel. Then he began with the same question he had asked before. "Are you looking for a job?"

"No, sir, I am looking for a career in federal law enforcement."

The other two agents began questioning me about everything—my Marine Corps service, weapons experience, contact sports in school, my workout routine, any illegal activities I might have been involved in, and my willingness to relocate.

They also posed many "what if" situations. "What would you do if . . . ?" I gave my opinion and course of action. This went on for hours. The process was grueling, but I would not quit.

I returned home exhausted. I wrote Agent Coates a note thanking him for his time and the interview. I had recently read that a person should send a thank-you note after an interview. As I was to learn, this was not always the right thing to do.

Days later, the phone rang. "This is Bobby Coates with the Secret Service. May I speak to Dan Emmett, please?"

"This is Dan Emmett, sir," I replied.

"I got your thank-you note. We don't go in for that sort of thing at the Secret Service. I am thanked twice a month by the US government." He was referring to when he was paid.

At that point I thought my chances of being a Secret Service agent dropped to below zero. Sunk by a thank-you note!

After a pause, Agent Coates continued. "Come on down to the office and pick up your background information forms." Then the call ended. I traveled back to Atlanta that very day. I picked up the papers, completed them in record time, and returned them to the Atlanta field office. I went back to work at the bank and waited.

Nine months after my first interview, I was having a particularly long, boring day at my bank job. The phone rang.

"This is Bobby Coates, Secret Service."

"Yes, sir."

"I have a job for you in Charlotte, base pay thirteen thousand dollars per year, if you want it. Take a few minutes and call me back with an answer."

"I . . . I . . . I don't need to take a few minutes, sir. I would like to accept the position."

"I would like to have had you in Atlanta, but there are no openings. The opening in Charlotte is the only one available." Agent Coates continued, "You will have to pay for your own move to Charlotte, North Carolina. There are three possible report dates. The first date is May 16th. And . . ."

"I will be glad to report on May 16th, sir."

I didn't tell him I would have accepted the field office on Mars if offered. At last, I was on the way. I was going to be a Secret Service agent, partly because I had not given up.

NEW AGENT

"Hi, I am Dan Emmett. First day on the job." Eighteen months after my discharge from the Marine

Corps, I reported for duty at the Charlotte field office. The officer manager led me into the special agent in charge's office.

"Remain standing, Mr. Emmett. Raise your right hand."

Then the SAIC administered the oath of office. I knew the oath well. It was exactly the same one I had taken years earlier as a marine officer.

I, (state name of enlistee), do solemnly swear (or affirm) that I will support and defend the Constitution of the United States against all enemies, foreign and domestic; that I will bear true faith and allegiance to the same; and that I will obey the orders of the President of the United States and the orders of the officers appointed over me, according to regulations and the Uniform Code of Military Justice. So help me God.

After my swearing in and a lecture on the duties, responsibilities, and work ethic of the Secret Service, an agent took me to another room. They fingerprinted me and took my official Secret Service photo. This picture would appear in the coveted Commission Book I would carry throughout my career.

On my first day as an agent, I met Frank, a firearms

instructor and one of the oldest agents still on the job. Early in his career, Frank had worked on the protection detail for President Dwight D. (Ike) Eisenhower. The president enjoyed playing golf. Frank walked golf courses with President Eisenhower while carrying a Thompson submachine gun in a golf bag.

Frank instructed me in the use of a Smith & Wesson standard-issue revolver to prepare me for the upcoming special agent training. Frank and I drove to the Charlotte Police Academy firing range. When we got there, Frank said, "This is not a combat course. This is a Standard Qualification Course where you will be shooting at bullseye targets. It is designed to test you on the basics of shooting."

I was to fire the Smith & Wesson in single action shooting. This meant I was to pull the hammer back to cock the pistol before firing each round. The course required only thirty shots.

"Okay, the first time you do a dry run," said Frank.

"Why no ammunition?" I questioned.

He simply said, "It will help you get the feel of it."

He nodded toward the gun. I did as instructed. I did not mention to Frank I had been firing handguns since I was thirteen. In fact, I had been the top shooter with a .45 pistol in my marine unit.

After practicing, Frank gave me live ammunition. "Good luck!" he said with a smile.

I scored 290 out of a possible 300. Once I qualified on the Smith & Wesson, I received twelve rounds of .38 special+P+ammunition, a speedloader (which held six more rounds), and a holster. Now "armed and dangerous," I realized I was probably more dangerous to myself than anyone else.

The next week all the agents in North Carolina came together for quarterly firearms requalification. While at the training day, I qualified on the revolver, Uzi submachine gun, and Remington 870 shotgun. The firearms training and qualifying would prove to be some of the more exciting work in those first weeks.

NOT SO GLAMOROUS WORK

Everyone knows the Secret Service protects the president of the United States. What many forget is that until 2003 the Secret Service was a part of the Department of the Treasury. This means that much of the work involves government check fraud and counterfeiting. My field training began with check investigations in Western North Carolina. This was truly at the dull end of the Secret Service's work.

On my first day of working these cases, I accompanied a seasoned agent. We interviewed a few people who had reported forged checks. We took handwriting samples. Through good detective work we began to track people down. I quickly learned that the danger with forgers was not so much the forgers but with their dogs . . . a lesson I learned the hard way.

We pulled into a narrow dirt driveway. Paul, the agent training me, said, "Always *back* the car in, just in case something goes wrong. You can get out quickly if you have to."

Paul wore a sports jacket and pants. I, unfortunately, stood out like a sore thumb in a three-piece suit. I thought it made me look more official. I decided to dress differently in the future.

As we got out of the car, I could hear trouble coming with the bark of dogs. A large, mud-caked mongrel rounded the mobile home.

"The dog don't bite," said the owner rather calmly.

He did not say anything about whether the dog would jump all over a newly minted agent in a brand-new three-piece suit. The dog came straight for me and put muddy paws all over my "official" looking new clothes.

"We are with the United States Secret Service," Paul said as we displayed our Commission Books with badges. "We are investigating check fraud and need a sample of your signature."

The dog's owner agreed to give us handwriting samples. As I slid a form in front of the man, a large drop of tobacco juice dripped from his mouth, staining the form. Seeing my quiet but noticeable disgust, Paul held back his comments. When we got back into the car, Paul burst out laughing. "Everyone has to pay their dues, rookie! Welcome to the glamorous world of the Secret Service!"

The main work of small field offices is cases like this one. I quickly realized that if I was ever going to be on a presidential protection detail, I had to do whatever type of work I was ordered to do and do it well. I did not realize how my attitude would change with agent training school.

SPECIAL AGENT TRAINING

Training is constant. An agent is ALWAYS being trained. From the beginning of my career to my retirement, I received training. In addition to never-ending on-the-job training, each new agent has six months of intensive formal training. This training occurs in two phases—criminal investigations and protective detail training. These are conducted at two different sites.

The Criminal Investigative Training Program (CITP) is at the Federal Law Enforcement Training Center in Brunswick, Georgia. There, a new agent learns the basics common to all federal law enforcement agencies. The courses are designed to certify all federal agents in criminal investigation, not just the Secret Service. The basics include firearm training, physical fitness, and defensive measures. The most important part of this training is learning how to conduct a criminal investigation from the beginning all the way to the courtroom.

After graduation from CITP, the Secret Service agent trainee attends the Secret Service Special Agent Training Course (SATC) at the James J. Rowley Training Center in Laurel, Maryland. Primarily Secret Service agents are trained at this facility along with uniformed division officers. The new agent learns how to provide executive protection for the president and others to whom they are assigned. Also, the agent is taught criminal investigation procedures specific to the Secret Service. The training is extensive.

The most intense segment of training is firearms. All agents are experts in ALL issued weapons. Hours are spent on the firing range practicing with the revolver, Remington shotgun, and UZI submachine gun. In addition to hitting the target, moving or still, an agent must know how the weapon works.

Almost every day during my training, fellow agents and I fired hundreds of rounds of ammunition. By the end of the week, each man could scarcely hold a gun. Shoulders grew sore and faces swollen from the recoil of 12-gauge shotguns with sharp metal folding stocks.

All in my class were super-competitive. There was no such thing as a relaxed day of shooting. In any course of fire, revolver, submachine gun, or shotgun, we all tried our best to outdo each other.

While practicing a counter to a rear chokehold, I unintentionally dislocated my partner's elbow. Everyone in the room heard a loud pop. My friend went pale. His elbow was not in the right place. They took him to the hospital where his elbow was relocated. He returned to the session.

Emergency Medical Technicians (EMT), along

with other experts in the medical community, instructed us in being a First Responder. We learned to answer any medical emergency—from heart attacks to delivering a baby. This training saved many lives over the years.

Each day included challenging physical training—running, climbing, lifting weights, exercising. A new agent learned and practiced aggressive defensive tactics DAILY. Because I had endured marine training, the Secret Service training served to renew and refresh that previous work.

As training progressed, we came to know and understand each other's strengths and weaknesses. We became like family—a family that worked, played, and sometimes fought together—but family. We might argue among ourselves, but woe to the poor soul who trifled with any man in my class. To push one of us was to push all.

Upon graduation from both required beginning training sessions (two eight-week courses), new Secret Service agents are prepared for any situation that might occur in the course of their career. This means everything from a gunfight to subduing a resisting suspect; from stopping arterial bleeding to the all-important covering and evacuating the president in the event of an attack. Graduation does not signal the end of training for an agent. Throughout their career, an agent receives refresher training in protection, firearms, computers, investigation, the law, and anything else that is needed.

As I worked in the Charlotte field office mostly in check fraud investigations, I occasionally got to work on temporary protection details or to stand post on a presidential visit to some city.

FIRST PRESIDENTIAL POST

Only weeks after returning to the Charlotte field office from my training, I volunteered to go to Atlanta to stand post while President Ronald Reagan visited the city. I liked Atlanta and wanted to be in on protecting the president. Even though I was not on the PPD, at least I would be assisting the PPD in their work. Also, I would not be investigating check fraud.

The actual work was nothing exciting. I stood post in an underground parking garage with orders to let no one come through. I watched empty vehicles to make sure no one placed an explosive charge on or under them. I never even saw the president or any of his PPD. While there, I saw five very fit-looking agents sitting in a Mercury station wagon with M16 rifles and semiautomatic pistols. These guys were a Secret Service Counter Assault Team (CAT).

CAT is one of the special, or tactical, teams of the Secret Service. It is made of agents whose mission is to respond to any organized attack on the president with speed, surprise, and violence of action. I had heard about CAT but knew little about the program.

I walked over to the Mercury for a better look. I talked with the agent in the rear of the vehicle. Like me, he was a former marine. After only a few minutes conversation with him, I was so impressed I decided that I wanted to be on CAT for my next assignment when I left Charlotte. The CAT agent handed me a piece of paper with information and an application. He told me to fill it out when I got back to the office and send it to him.

What I did not understand at the time of our talk was that an agent had to have served for at least two years. CAT would have to wait for the time being, but it was without doubt the next thing in my sights for my career.

MY FIRST PRESIDENTIAL ENCOUNTER

Not long after, I had another chance to stand post on a detail protecting President Reagan. Most new Secret Service agents are initially a bit starstruck when first coming into the presence of the president of the United States. I must admit that as worldly as I considered myself to be as a former Marine Corps officer, I became one of those agents.

Ronald Reagan was president when I entered the Secret Service in 1983 and was already an American icon. Prior to becoming the president, he had been a motion picture star and the governor of California. He also survived an assassination attempt that nearly killed him and three other people. One of those wounded was a Secret Service agent. During and after this attempt on the president's life, the Secret Service was in the national headlines almost as much as the president himself.

While too junior to be a member of Reagan's PPD, I stood many hours on middle and outer perimeter posts during several of his trips. While on post, I dreamed of being one of the select few agents who stood within arm's length of the president of the United States. I strongly wanted to do more than stand post for him. On most of these assignments I was so far removed from the action I seldom even saw the president.

Consequently, I recall my first encounter with Reagan vividly. I had been a Secret Service agent for a very short time when I received instructions to report to Nashville, Tennessee, to the Grand Ole Opry where President Reagan was to speak at the birthday celebration of country music legend Roy Acuff. This was going to be a huge event and promised to be an interesting assignment. Along with the president's visit, country music stars would be walking around everywhere.

According to my orders, I reported to the briefing room at the Grand Ole Opry at the appointed date and time to receive my assignment. Expecting the usual obscure post, I could hardly believe my good luck. I was assigned the holding room. This is a great assignment no matter who the protectee is for one huge reason. Instead of standing for hours upon end in one spot, the holding room agent was allowed to *sit down* until the arrival of POTUS. The holding room is generally the first place the president goes upon arrival at a site. The main purpose of the post was to ensure the security of the room prior to the president's arrival.

This time the holding room was Roy Acuff's

dressing room itself! Upon being posted inside Mr. Acuff's room by the PPD site agent, I sat back in a comfortable seat and enjoyed my good fortune. About two hours later I heard over my radio the news of the president's arrival and pending approach. I quickly stood up to take my post in front of the room's door.

I bristled when I heard something in the distance. At first it was a muted rumble that grew louder and louder with each second. The sound seemed to be a thousand footsteps thundering down the hallways of the Opry. As I looked toward the noise of shoes impacting tile mixed with the sound of many voices speaking at once, I realized this was the president's entourage. Trying to look my most professional, I guarded the door with all the swagger I could muster until the lead PPD agent with President Reagan bumped me aside and said, "Thanks, we have it."

At this point my primary assignment was finished. I then picked up my secondary assignment—to guard the giant birthday cake sitting backstage. As boring and ridiculous as the post seemed, it was actually important in that the president was probably going to have some birthday cake with Roy Acuff, and it therefore had to be guarded. We also serve to protect the cake.

The backstage area of the Grand Ole Opry was dimly lit as I relieved the agent who had been given the monumental task of protecting the cake prior to my arrival. He said, "Good luck" as he walked away.

I replied a bit sarcastically, "No one is going to assassinate this cake as long as I am protecting it!"

As I stood in the near darkness of the backstage area, my mind began to wander a bit as I thought about driving back to Charlotte. I daydreamed of the upcoming weekend's possibilities. Suddenly I sensed someone standing very close to me. I turned to see who dared approach Roy Acuff's birthday cake so closely and was met with the famous smile of Ronald Wilson Reagan, fortieth president of the United States. The president stood no more than one foot from me!

Alongside president Reagan was his agent in charge who was also smiling. This was a moment that could not be possibly happening. Then it became even more unbelievable. President Reagan looked directly at me and said, "Well, what do you think?"

The president of the United States spoke to me! My mind went into high gear. Obviously, a clever, well-thought-out response was called for.

Trying to keep my voice under control, I replied, "I think it's a great cake, Mr. President."

Then as quickly as he had appeared, he and his agent in charge were gone. As I stood in the near darkness, I wondered out loud to myself, "Did that actually just happen?"

At that moment another agent appeared and assumed the responsibility of the guarding of the cake, and I moved to my next assignment—a seated post in the Opry auditorium. I could actually watch part of the program as I conducted general crowd observation.

After the president's on-stage remarks, Lee Greenwood appeared alongside President Reagan and sang "God Bless the USA." His rendition of that song while standing with President Reagan brought the house down. To this day, I am not embarrassed to recall that I had to wipe more than one tear away as I listened to the words. I am also not embarrassed to admit that now, all these years later, that song still evokes those emotions and the memories of that day of my first encounter with POTUS—Ronald Wilson Reagan.

★ 4 ★

Protection

Amid the mud-caked dogs and check fraud investigations in Charlotte, I was assigned to temporary protection details. These assignments were closer to what I had imagined I would do as an agent. In these years in North Carolina, I learned more about this amazing federal agency.

The Secret Service did not seem to be much of a secret. Everyone knows that the Secret Service protects the president of the United States. Even as a kid, I knew THAT. As I prepared for my interview to become an agent, I had studied the history of the Secret Service. I decided to do my homework to be ready. During my training as a new agent at the SATC I learned even more. I was surprised at what I discovered.

On the very afternoon before he was killed, Abraham Lincoln signed into law the agency that would eventually become responsible for protecting presidents. That evening, John Wilkes Booth shot Abraham Lincoln while the president and his wife watched a play at Ford's Theater. However, the Secret Service's first purpose was not to protect presidents. The first mission of the agency was to prevent people from making fake money illegally (counterfeiting).

Counterfeiting was a huge problem before and during the Civil War. At that time the states issued money—bills and coins. It was easy to copy this money since there were so many different kinds in use. In the mid-to-late 1800s, it was thought that more than one-third of the nation's money was fake! The Secret Service was created to stop this.

I realized in my research about the agency that it would be thirty-six years after Lincoln signed the original law, before the duty of protecting the president was added to the mission of the Secret Service. Unfortunately, two other presidents would be assassinated before this protection began.

I remembered from my American history classes

in high school and college that Abraham Lincoln, James Garfield, and William McKinley had all been assassinated while serving as president. I did not know that even before Lincoln was killed there had been two other attempts on presidents' lives.

The first of these happened at the Capitol building in Washington, DC, on a damp winter day. President Andrew Jackson, sometimes called "Old Hickory," was leaving the funeral of a congressman when a gunman jumped from the crowd gathered on the Capitol steps. The assassin pulled a single-shot pistol from his cloak and aimed it at the heart of the president who stood only thirty feet away. Before anyone could react, the would-be killer pulled the trigger. The percussion cap made a loud "crack" but the powder in the gun did not fire.

Several people, including President Jackson, moved toward the man who quickly pulled a second pistol from his cloak and tried to fire a second time. The same thing happened. The percussion cap exploded without igniting the gun. A navy lieutenant knocked the man down while others restrained him. I smiled when I read one account. In that group who subdued the man, was none other than Davy Crockett of Tennessee. He was a congressman at the time.

I also learned that the second attempt was on

Abraham Lincoln himself. It occurred nine months before Booth killed him. Lincoln did not have Secret Service protection since the agency had not been created yet. He did, however, have a cavalry troop that rode with him. Lincoln did not like all the attention and preferred to ride by himself. It was told that Lincoln said he was "more afraid of being shot by the accidental discharge of one of the carbines or revolvers (of new recruits) than of any attempt on my life."

The initial, unsuccessful attempt on Lincoln's life happened late one August evening. Lincoln was riding alone from Washington to his summerhouse, The Soldier's Home, on the outskirts of the city. As he neared the gate to The Soldier's Home, a shot rang out. Lincoln's horse, Old Abe, bolted. Lincoln said that the horse took off "with one reckless bound he unceremoniously separated me from my eight-dollar plug-hat, with which I parted company without any assent, expressed or implied."

Lincoln and Old Abe galloped into The Soldier's Home and were greeted by Private Nichols. The private questioned the president about his missing hat. Lincoln explained about the shot and the runaway horse. Later Nichols and a friend searched for the hat and found it with a bullet hole in it.

Lincoln did not take this incident too seriously,

saying, "Now, in the face of this testimony in favor of your theory of danger to me, personally, I can't bring myself to believe that any one has shot or will deliberately shoot at me with the purpose of killing me; although I must acknowledge that I heard this fellow's bullet whistle at an uncomfortably short distance from these headquarters of mine."

In my studies, I found a whole list of attempts on presidents' lives. And yet at its beginning, the Secret Service was a part of the Department of the Treasury. It was created to stop counterfeiting. This mission later developed into investigating any money deception involving the government including checks and online fraud. This part of the purpose of the Secret Service is what I worked on at the Charlotte field office and later in New York City. Financial crimes are still very much an important segment of the work of the Secret Service.

With the assassination of James Garfield in 1881 and then William McKinley only twenty years later, Congress decided to add presidential protection to the work of the Secret Service. This is when the Secret Service got the job that I knew the most about— guarding the president of the United States (POTUS).

Vice President Theodore Roosevelt, a man I have admired for most of my life, became the first president to receive protection from the Secret Service. Roosevelt, who lived an active life, was on a camping trip in the Adirondack Mountains of New York State when President McKinley was shot. At first, everyone thought the president would recover from his wound. However, eight days later, McKinley died and Theodore Roosevelt was sworn in as the twenty-sixth president of the United States.

At age forty-two, Roosevelt is the youngest person to be president. He was active and felt he did not want to be shadowed by bodyguards. I like him because he boldly tried to do many things—soldier, cowboy, police chief, writer, hunter, governor, and president. The first Presidential Protection Detail (both men—yes that means TWO) stood watch at the White House and traveled with the president.

William Craig, a 6-foot-4, 280-pound Scotsman who had served in the British army, followed President Roosevelt everywhere. Only months after receiving the assignment to protect the president, he died on a protection detail. He was the first Secret Service agent to be killed in the line of duty.

Craig always rode with the president. While in Pittsfield, Massachusetts, Craig joined Roosevelt, Governor Winthrop Crane, and presidential secretary George Cortelyou in a horse-drawn carriage. As the carriage progressed through the town, an electric trolley car struck the presidential carriage. Craig was crushed in the accident. Roosevelt said, "The man who was killed was one of whom I was fond and whom I greatly prized for his loyalty and faithfulness."

I also learned the names of others who died in various ways while on duty. Only two died while serving on a Presidential Protection Division (PPD)—William Craig and White House police officer Leslie Coffelt. Their deaths did not deter me from wanting to serve in the Secret Service on a PPD working shift.

Leslie Coffelt's sacrifice came only a few years before I was born. He was standing outside Blair House in Washington, DC, where President Harry Truman lived while the White House was being renovated. One November afternoon, two men rushed Blair House mortally wounding Coffelt. Though seriously injured, Coffelt steadied himself and fired at the attackers killing one of them. Coffelt died a few hours later. Coffelt is the only officer shot and killed while protecting a US president.

The stories of these men inspired me to do my work as a Secret Service agent. Even though I began work investigating financial crimes against the government, I wanted to be on the PPD.

A SPECIAL TEMPORARY PROTECTION ASSIGNMENT

The president may assign Secret Service protection to anyone he wishes. This type of detail is usually comprised of agents from various field offices like Charlotte where I was serving. These small details only last for a few days to a few weeks. During these assignments, junior agents learn the protection business. It is also where reality hits young, idealistic junior agents. They begin to understand, contrary to popular belief, that protection is anything but glamorous. It is very demanding work that requires a great deal of strength and watchfulness.

During the final thirty days of the 1984 presidential campaign, President Reagan directed that Senator Edward (Ted) Kennedy was to receive Secret Service protection. Kennedy campaigned for Democratic nominee Walter Mondale, who was running against President Reagan. Senator Kennedy was the last living son of Joseph and Rose Kennedy. Two of the Kennedys' sons, John and Robert, died by assassin's bullets. A third, Joe, died when an explosive detonated prematurely in his plane in World War II. President Reagan signed an order of protection in October, granting Kennedy Secret Service protection until the end of the campaign on Election Day the next month.

Just over a year out of agent school and still assigned to Charlotte, I volunteered for this temporary protection detail. I was happy to be on the road for what turned out to be a very interesting thirty days with the senator. All the fifteen agents selected for this assignment were similar to me—young, male, single, and not concerned with how long the assignment lasted.

This was a high-profile assignment due to the fact we were protecting Senator Kennedy, President John Kennedy's younger brother. Before we began our duties with the senator, the entire detail returned to the Secret Service Training Center in Maryland for a day of protective detail training.

The protective detail with Senator Kennedy was tough. We worked thirty straight days without a day off. Often we visited several cities in one day. I would wake up in a dark hotel room with zero idea of what city or state I was in.

My shift started at midnight. I watched over the senator until 8:00 a.m. He traveled to a new city each day. We sometimes were relieved early at 6:00 a.m. by the day shift. We scrambled to pack, get a cab, and rush to an airport for a flight to the next city. After arriving, we made a beeline to our hotel, where normally we found our rooms not ready. We slept in hotel lobbies until rooms were available. We would sleep three or four hours and begin the process all over again.

I learned that friendly crowds could be more dangerous than hostile ones. Friendly crowds tend to move like a human wave toward a popular person. A rope line or five young agents cannot always stop this force of nature.

Everywhere we went in Massachusetts enormous crowds appeared. These people paid little attention to rope lines surrounding the stage. Most of the "offenders" were ancient, blue-haired ladies. Due to the gender and age of our intruders, we did not employ our usual tactics. We simply formed a human shield around the senator and hoped no one poked him in the eye with a pen while seeking an autograph.

Patrick, Senator Kennedy's youngest son, came on a number of these trips. The older crowd loved Patrick. On one occasion, Patrick was wearing one of his Uncle Jack's PT-109 tie clasps. President John Kennedy gave these away during his brief time in office. The tie clasps were quite valuable, not to mention the sentimental value it held for Patrick.

In one rope line encounter, these women overran Patrick. His hair was tousled. His clothing rumpled. It looked like he had just rolled out of bed. His tie was almost ripped from his neck. Patrick's heirloom tie clasp was taken in the press of the crowd. I felt badly about Patrick's loss of his PT-109 tie clasp. Five agents cannot hold back a tide of elderly groupies.

Senator Kennedy always cooperated with his protection detail. He understood the process. He had been around the Secret Service since 1960 when his brother was elected president. Twenty years later he had a protective detail when he ran for president himself. The senator always told us his plans. He let us know of any changes. Our job was to protect him, and he helped us do that.

On this assignment we spent several days in Los Angeles and Hollywood. Senator Kennedy campaigned by day and by night. The Hollywood elite—movie stars, directors, and producers—hosted a never-ending series of parties. Some functions lasted well into the early-morning hours.

As famous and wealthy as these people were, many found it more interesting to sip a drink and talk to a Secret Service agent than to associate with fellow actors. Sometimes their interest in our work made it difficult to do our work. Once I was surrounded by a group of actors, each asking questions about protecting the president. Though big name stars interacted with us in different ways, most acknowledged our presence.

One young actor who was about to play a Secret Service agent in an upcoming movie asked for pointers. He was very appreciative and wanted to know if there was anything he could do for us. We answered yes and asked that he tell his producer and director that, contrary to most Hollywood efforts, real Secret Service agents do not wear sunglasses indoors.

One evening I was standing post outside the senator's hotel room with strict orders to allow no one to enter. Suddenly Oscar-winning actor Gregory Peck appeared. Mr. Peck was early for a party in the senator's suite. He was tall and his persona matched the one portrayed on the screen. He smiled pleasantly at me. I felt as if General McArthur or Captain Ahab was standing before me.

"Good evening, Mr. Peck," I said as I knocked on the door. I was not going to make "General McArthur" wait to see Ted Kennedy.

Senator Kennedy did not like to fly on small airplanes. He had been in a crash when he was younger. Several were killed in the crash that broke Kennedy's back. Unfortunately for the senator, most of the little towns in which he campaigned were accessible only by small plane. Kennedy flew to all these places, but was not a fan.

At the end of the campaign just before the election, we flew on an old DC-3 to Senator Kennedy's home at Hyannis, Massachusetts. The airplane was ancient but dependable. The weather was deplorable with low clouds, rain, and wind. We landed safely but I noticed that the senator was ghostly pale and quickly exited the plane.

The Kennedy compound at Hyannis Port impressed me with its New England elegance. The main house had once belonged to the patriarch of the family, Ambassador Joseph P. Kennedy. Another house had been the late Robert F. Kennedy's. The late President John F. Kennedy had owned a large gray-shingled Cape Cod nearby.

I saw the house every day and was aware it had belonged to President Kennedy. I just assumed it was an empty house that had been the summer home of the thirty-fifth president of the United States.

On the last day of our assignment, Senator Kennedy hosted a party to express thanks to the Secret Service agents who had protected him for the last month. The senator came dressed in a blue denim shirt with a black warm-up jacket and a shock of disheveled, graying hair. This was not his typical look.

He set aside his usual reserve and was the perfect host. He encouraged us to have more lobster and beer. Most of us did not need encouragement even though we were dead tired and looking forward to going home. Late in the afternoon, people began to depart for the airport and other destinations.

"Would anyone like to tour my brother's house?" the senator asked those who remained. He looked directly at me. "How about you, Dan?"

"Yes, sir," I replied. "I would enjoy seeing the president's house."

The senator escorted three of us to the back door of President Kennedy's house. He casually explained that the house was largely in the same condition as when the president had lived there. I thought he meant the furniture and the drapes were the same. I had no idea how accurate his statement was.

I expected the senator to give us a brief tour through the house. Instead, he handed me the key and said, "Here, Dan, please lock it up when you are done." Then he left. He moved toward the main house with the posture and gait of a much older man. It was clear that the years after the assassinations of his brothers,

President John Kennedy and Senator Robert Kennedy, had done little to relieve his pain. He still grieved.

During my time with him, he seemed a man tormented by the tragedies that had occurred in his life. Secret Service agents are with those they protect all the time. Agents see politicians in ways that no others do. Sometimes the view is tragic.

We stepped into the house. I was shocked. It was as though the house had never received word of President Kennedy's death. All was frozen in time for twenty-one years!

The other two agents and I explored the old house that was scented with a hint of dampness from the late New England autumn. The house seemed much like any other. The furnishings ranged from antique through the early 1960s. The clue that this house was *not* like others lay in the reading materials, in the *Life* magazines and newspapers lying on tables. We realized that all had been printed in 1963 or earlier.

The other two agents had to leave pretty soon. I probably should have left with them. However, I was not ready to end this once-in-a-lifetime opportunity. Now alone, I moved through a museum's worth of President Kennedy's personal belongings. It was as if I had traveled back in time to November 21, 1963, the day before President Kennedy's assassination.

I was surrounded by an abundance of priceless items. I looked at framed photographs of President Kennedy and his family. The closet was filled with the president's business suits on wooden hangers seemingly waiting for Kennedy to return and wear them again.

I stood alone in President Kennedy's bedroom. My surroundings darkened in the fading afternoon light. As I was about to depart the bedroom and the house that time forgot, two items on the bureau caught my attention. When I moved closer for a better look, I found a pair of gold cuff links. The cuff links, like the house, seemed to be waiting for their owner to return.

The initials "JFK" were engraved in the gold cuff links. These had belonged to President John F. Kennedy. It struck me that these had been resting on the dresser since 1963. They were most likely last touched by President Kennedy himself. I resisted the urge to examine them more closely.

In addition to entrusting the Secret Service with his life, Senator Ted Kennedy had also trusted us to tour the home and leave it untouched. The handling of these treasures would have been unprofessional. I was not a tourist but a trained Secret Service agent. From the first day of my career, I was taught to respect the personal lives and property of those I protected.

Leaving the cuff links in their resting place, I thought of how much the senator trusted us. I exited the house and looked for the senator. I discovered him walking along the beach in front of the compound.

When I handed him the key, he said, "Thank you Dan, I appreciate your work and that of the Secret Service very much."

"Thank you, Senator, for allowing us the honor of viewing the president's home," I replied.

"Where do you live, Dan?"

"Charlotte, North Carolina, but I am from Gainesville, Georgia."

"How long have you been with the Secret Service?"

"Only eighteen months after serving as a marine officer for four years."

We talked for a few more minutes. After a pause in the conversation, I sensed that he wanted to be alone. We shook hands, and I left him standing on the beach staring out at the ocean. In these moments I was reminded of that afternoon in the third grade when I had heard the news of President Kennedy's assassination. I renewed my resolve to protect the lives of those important to our country.

It had been a long thirty days for Senator Kennedy as well as me. I left for the airport, home, and new assignments.

TO CAT OR NOT

I became convinced that I wanted to work on the Counter Assault Team (CAT). After three years in Charlotte it looked like I would be assigned to CAT training. Much to my disappointment, this did not work out. I was transferred to the New York City field office.

This transfer was not to a plum assignment. Even though I had over three years' experience and had worked all types of cases assigned to the Secret Service, I began working forged checks in New York. The contrast between working these cases in North Carolina and New York City was off the scale. In New York both the landscape and the criminal were different.

We had to enter some of the most horrid tenement

slums in the country. There were times I had to step over human feces in the hallways as well as unconscious humans. No mud-caked dogs there. When we entered these apartments we met another menace—the cockroach.

In some apartments the walls were alive with these insects. Closets and kitchens were infested. One did not dare lean against a wall or touch anything. In addition to dropping on you, these nuisances crawled up your leg and took refuge. The first thing I did when I got home was to completely undress down to my underwear in the hallway of my residence. More than once, after I had shaken out my clothes, a roach would drop to the ground and then be murdered by me.

The New York office had many investigations, but protection always won out over them. Since the United Nations is in NYC, we were often pulled off investigation work to protect visiting dignitaries. I liked this work, but many of my coworkers did not. They preferred investigating financial crimes.

In spite of the working conditions, we always managed to make the best of things. One very hot summer day I was supposed to watch a residence in the Bronx from inside a surveillance van. Joe, our Office Support Technician (OST), was in charge of all electronic and vehicular surveillance equipment.

Joe had been born in China but was a US citizen and long-time resident of NYC. He was small and compact in stature. Even though Joe was one of the nicest guys I had ever known, he was a genuine badass. He held black belts in various martial arts. Joe could kill a man in seconds using only his hands and feet. In addition to working for the Secret Service, Joe also partly owned the best Chinese restaurant in New York.

One day, I was behind the curtain in a van with Joe at the wheel. He parked the van across the street from the target location. He left the vehicle and walked down the street to observe the house. I stayed in the locked van to watch the house through a side porthole. As time passed, the temperature in the van climbed past 100 degrees. I was shirtless and soaked in sweat. Every ten minutes Joe would call me on the radio to check on my status.

"It is getting rather hot in here," I said.

"I will bring you something to drink," Joe promised.

About ten minutes later, I heard the driver's door unlock. Joe appeared with a paper bag containing what I assumed was water.

"Thanks, Joe." Then I looked into the bag to find

not water but a six-pack of Heineken. "Uh, Joe. You know we are on duty. I can't drink this."

"You do realize that in my culture it is an insult to refuse such a kind gift," he said with a rather mysterious look.

Realizing my error, I mumbled, "Thank you, Joe." I opened a beer and drank deeply from the green can. It was the best-tasting beer of my life.

After a few hours, we left the scene. Joe insisted that we go to his restaurant in Chinatown. We entered through the back door, where Joe was treated as royalty. Speaking in Chinese, he introduced me to the staff. We sat at the best table in the house. I was definitely in the minority as the only Caucasian in the place. Joe ordered for us. I dined on the best-tasting food imaginable. I later learned that to be Joe's guest at his place was a great honor, afforded to few. That day will always stand out as my best day in New York.

★ 5 ★

CAT

I had been up to my knees in cockroaches, rats, and the New York field office for two years. I was weary of the work there. One Thursday, while working through an investigative file, the assistant to the special agent in charge called me into his office.

"The Counter Assault Team School is to start on Monday," he said. "It seems that at the last minute a candidate backed out. This leaves an open slot. They need it filled right now." He paused. "Do you want to go?"

"Yes," I instantly replied. "I can go." I had learned plenty. Now my time of paying dues was over.

Five years after becoming a Secret Service agent, I was on my way to Counter Assault Team training. With no advance warning, I found myself headed for the most physically demanding school in the Secret Service. Some had doubts as to my readiness, but I did not.

Most marines, current or former, exist in a perpetual state of physical readiness. But since the opportunity came at the last minute, was I ready? All my future classmates had the advantage of attending the pre-selection course a few weeks earlier. I could have used some time to catch up but there was none. I was notified on a Friday to report to training on the following Monday. They had been physically working out in preparation for the selection course. I would need to catch up.

The physical fitness test presented the first hurdle to becoming a CAT agent. Failing only one event on the test caused an agent to wash out. To pass the test a student had to successfully complete a sequence of:

1. 10 dead-hang pull-ups
2. 40 perfect locked-out push-ups in 1 minute
3. 40 perfectly formed sit-ups in 1 minute

4. 1.5-mile run in less than 10 minutes and
   30 seconds
5. 10 dead-hang pull-ups
6. 40 perfect locked-out push-ups in
   1 minute

Form was critical in each event. Any repetition that did not meet the standards of the instructor's staff simply was not counted. At the conclusion of the run, the candidates returned to the gym to repeat all the upper-body events. Only this time, the pull-ups were done using the opposite hand position than in the first set. For example, if the first time palms faced out, then palms had to face in for the second round.

I had been training for this test my entire adult life without knowing it. In the Marine Corps, pull-ups and running were the two main areas of fitness. All marines feel as if they were born on a pull-up bar. Even though I did not have a pull-up bar at home on which to practice, I improvised by using the back of a stair in the stairwell of my apartment building.

I had worked out each day on those stairs for the past two years, and now my time had come. When my turn came to do pull-ups, I was so jacked up with adrenaline I practically vaulted to the ceiling on the first rep. I followed perfect form. I did the ten pull-ups overhanded in slow motion, coming to a complete dead hang for a least one second.

The push-ups and sit-ups were easy. Next was the run. I exploded off the starting line like a Thoroughbred at the Kentucky Derby. I reached the halfway point in almost record time but had expended nearly all of my energy. I was so depleted that I almost failed the run! I finished in 10:20. Only ten seconds separated me from continuing in the program or going home. Too close! I vowed to pace myself a little better for the rest of the school.

WEAPONS QUALIFICATION

Although longer today, in 1988 CAT school lasted three weeks. Each week consisted of six, twelve-hour workdays. Weapons qualification presented the most difficult section of the training. The standard Secret Service agent qualified with a 210 out of a possible 300 points for each issued weapon. CAT agents, on the other hand, were required to score a minimum of 270 out of the possible 300 (90 percent) with the M16 rifle, MP5 submachine gun, and the Sig Sauer pistol.

The CAT courses of fire called for almost impossible time requirements along with multiple magazine changes. This required near-perfect motor skills. Failure to meet qualifications with only one weapon meant total failure in the course. For CAT students, failure to qualify meant going home without a graduation certificate. For operational CAT agents who came for requalification, failure on one weapon meant leaving the program. In CAT, weapons proficiency was everything!

The M16 rifle and MP5 submachine gun course of fire consisted of sixty rounds within eighty seconds of facing a target. At one hundred yards, the CAT student fired ten rounds while standing. The student then executed a magazine change while dropping to a kneeling position. Ten more rounds. Another magazine change while changing to a prone position. Ten more rounds.

The student swiftly advanced to the fifty-yard line to fire five rounds standing and then dropped to the kneeling position for five more rounds. The final phase was from the five-yard line. The student fired a magazine of ten rounds, two rounds at a time within three seconds each time as he faced the automatic targets. This was followed by another magazine change, and then ten more rounds were fired on full automatic in bursts of two to three rounds. Failure to fire all rounds in the allotted time resulted in five points deducted for each saved round. Thirty points was the maximum that could be dropped.

The pistol course of fire was also challenging. The last six rounds were fired from fifty yards. Anyone who has fired a handgun can appreciate the difficulty of hitting a human torso-sized target from a distance equal to half a football field. Yet, every CAT agent is capable of doing this.

The goal in CAT firearms training is to be completely accurate while laying down a heavy volume of fire and to have the motor skills to conduct magazine changes in no time flat. Through firing thousands of rounds and going through hundreds of magazine changes, the skills became imbedded in the muscle memory. In a crisis, when there is no time to think, training takes over.

Learning to quickly clear a malfunctioning weapon is also a critical part of training. We practiced clearing stoppages until our hands bled. A CAT agent's primary weapon is the Colt M4 carbine, a variation of the M16 rifle. If just one of these weapons malfunctions the team is down one rifle. This could be the difference between success or failure; life or death.

The standard M4 malfunction drill begins by slapping the magazine base with the heel of the shooting hand. This ensures that the magazine is properly seated and the top round is in the proper position. M4 magazines usually have sharp edges that slice the palm of the hand. Students repeated this drill until the instructor felt the response was automatic. (This might mean repeating it fifty times!)

After raw flesh was exposed due to repeated magazine slaps, the student knew push-ups on pavement with a bleeding hand were ahead. In the summer heat, with hands constantly exposed to dirt, grease, and solvent, everyone's shooting hand became swollen and infected. Gnats and all types of insects loved our bleeding hands and elbows.

Another training memento is the CAT tattoo. This occurs when a hot, expended cartridge casing ejects from a rifle and lands on the sweat-coated neck of the agent to the shooter's right. The hot piece of brass tends to stick to the skin. If it is not immediately removed, a second-degree burn results in a permanent reminder of the day's training. Twenty-five years after our training, a friend and classmate still has a scar on the left side of his neck.

CAT TACTICS

Firearms training began the day when we were most rested. In the afternoons, we conducted a never-ending series of immediate action drills. These drills prepared us to respond to an ambush both from a vehicle or a stationary position.

CAT teams are composed of several agents and each team works tirelessly training and practicing tactics to protect the president.

We conducted this training in a crawl, walk, and run. The teams practiced in every way possible. The groups practiced in slow motion using unloaded weapons. In half speed. In full speed. With empty weapons. With weapons loaded with blanks.

We practiced exiting from a vehicle. Each one of us learned to respond to the leader's commands and to move and work as a team. The one-word commands described the attack. "Left!" "Right!" "Front!" "Moving!"

By the third week of drilling these moves over and over, we shifted to the most dangerous training in the Secret Service. We ran immediate action drills using live ammunition. Students under stress carrying live weapons jumped in and out of moving vehicles with a round in the chamber.

This phase of CAT school washed out more than a few. The work requires strength and stamina but also clear thinking. You had to be more than tough. You had to be smart. Safe weapons handling had to be second nature. Violations like sweeping or pointing a live weapon at a fellow CAT student, or keeping a finger on the trigger before one was ready to fire resulted in a warning. A second violation spelled the end of training for the student. One mistake could be fatal.

In addition to live-fire exercises where the students fired live ammunition only feet from one another, CAT training involved being shot at. All CAT students stood three hundred yards downrange while an instructor fired an M1 Garand rifle within a few feet of where the student stood. The purpose was to acquaint the student with the sound of a bullet traveling directly toward him.

The bullet from a high-powered rifle travels faster than the speed of sound. Therefore, when being shot at, the first thing a person hears is not the sound of the weapon being fired, but the "crack" of the bullet. So the sound of being shot at is "crack" followed by "kaboom." The instructor firing the M1 was an expert rifleman. We were not concerned he would shoot us. He did seem to take delight in putting his rounds as close to us as possible. Close enough that we could feel the impact of the bullet kicking up dirt around us.

As the weeks passed, the long days wore on. Drills

became more difficult as knees swelled and raw elbows became infected. Tempers and emotions also escalated, as we were rubbed raw. CAT agents sometimes spend sixteen hours confined in a vehicle. Agents spend weeks on the road together. Each student is constantly under observation by instructors looking for a breakdown in emotions.

If a man is not a true team player who can get along with others under difficult conditions, he will not become a CAT agent. Some trainees had to work on this mental toughness as much as on tactics and shooting skills.

Finally, graduation arrived. I would at last leave New York and join the Counter Assault Teams. A new assignment lay ahead.

With the constant threat of attack on America by terrorists, the US Secret Service Counter Assault Team enjoys a reputation in the international law enforcement and counterterrorist communities as one of the most elite units of its kind in the world. I was now a part of this unit.

ON DUTY WITH CAT

In 1989, I reported for duty in Washington, DC, at the Counter Assault Team office. I prided myself in passing (surviving) CAT training. Now it was time to do my job. Officially, I began protecting the president of the United States (POTUS), George Herbert Walker Bush, America's forty-first president. On my first day with CAT, I reported to the special agent in charge.

He looked me over. "Welcome to CAT, Mr. Emmett. Congratulations on your scores in CAT school. We are glad to have you on our team."

"Thank you, sir."

"You are the new guy here. So I do not want to hear your voice for one full year. Do you understand?"

I nodded silently. He smiled. "That's the right answer."

The first days, weeks, and months, I rode in the back of a black Suburban with a rear-window view of the world. My tactical duty was to provide a base of fire for the team in the event of an attack. Unofficially, my duties included always having my team leader's personal gear bag available. Also, I stacked the gear bags of the rest of the team in a neat and accessible manner.

Protecting the president is CAT's main function. However upon request, CAT accompanied the vice president on foreign trips where the threat level was high. Only two weeks after I began at CAT, I was assigned to the detail protecting Vice President Dan Quayle on a trip to the Far East. My first foreign journey took me to Seoul, South Korea.

As we drove through the busy city and bustling traffic, we totally controlled intersections and the route. In Korea, many people travel by motorcycle. One motorcycle somehow got into the motorcade. The biker, who wore a backpack, was traveling parallel to the motorcade. He accelerated as if he were coming up to the CAT truck and vice presidential limo, and then just as quickly backed off and dropped back.

It was not permissible to allow this unknown biker to pull past us and end up beside the VP limo. Once there, he could damage the limo and perhaps the vice president in any number of ways.

The motorcyclist approached a second time and looked as if he were going to pass us. My team leader calmly turned to me and said, "If he looks like he is going to go past us, take him out."

When the biker began to move closer to the CAT truck, I took aim with my M16. I placed the Ultra-Dot sight on his chest. The barrel of my weapon clearly protruded from the rear of the vehicle. Upon seeing my rifle aimed directly at him, the biker abruptly braked and moved out of the motorcade. Who he was or if he meant to harm the VP, we never knew. These types of incidents seemed to happen a lot in Asia, mostly due to the crazy way of driving found there. In our work, we always assumed the worst and prepared for it.

A TYPICAL DAY IN CAT

During my career, I was fortunate to have served in both the Presidential Protection Division (PPD) working shift as well as CAT, a section of PPD. I enjoyed my assignment on the PPD working shift immensely due to the front row seat it afforded me to history and the within arm's length proximity it afforded me to POTUS. However, without question, my most enjoyable assignment in twenty-one years was as a CAT agent.

CAT agents are fully qualified special agents of the United States Secret Service who have dual protective capabilities. They are qualified to work both as a Counter Assault Team agent as well as serve on a working shift surrounding POTUS. Without being disparaging to the outstanding men and women of PPD, an old saying in CAT was, "a CAT agent can work the shift, but a shift agent can't work CAT."

This became very apparent when PPD was short on manpower. They would borrow an agent or two from CAT while CAT could not borrow from PPD. Arrogant? Perhaps. But arrogance based upon undeniable fact. While outwardly humble, inside we knew our extensive training, high fitness level, and capabilities in weapons and tactics far exceeded the scope of a standard PPD agent. We were arguably the best protective agents in the Secret Service. That indisputable fact still holds true today. For the young hard-charging agent, it will always remain the place to be. In my view CAT is what all agents approaching the protective phase of their career should aspire to.

While CAT agents and PPD working shift agents both share responsibility for the protection of the president, the way in which they do so is entirely different. So is their daily routine. First, there is NO typical day in CAT. While each day consists of many repetitive responsibilities, the sequence is often different depending upon who is being protected. The primary mission of CAT is always to provide tactical protection of the president wherever he may be. Sometimes scheduling and circumstances require

CAT to move with the vice president or others such as high-level foreign heads of state.

Like an agent on PPD, a CAT agent works a normal shift each day when POTUS is in Washington. Those not engaged in operational work protecting POTUS are assigned to training. They engage in weapons requalification combined with tactical and physical training necessary to maintain their edge. All these skills are perishable and must be constantly practiced. The common denominator between CAT and their PPD counterparts is they both engage in an activity known to agents since 1902 when presidential protection began. It is the act of "waiting." Waiting in their truck, in a stairwell, or in an obscure location close enough to react to an attack on POTUS while remaining invisible. Silent, unseen, deadly, and far from glamorous, all agents would agree that CAT is completely essential to maintaining a safe environment for the president.

CAT has grown a great deal over the years, but manpower remains an issue. There is a continuous high demand for their skill set in situations other than PPD. CAT agents are in very high demand by almost every protective division in the Secret Service because having a CAT unit assigned to a protectee signifies its level of importance. If CAT is in the motorcade, your protectee is high level. If not, it is a gentleman's detail.

WITH THE VICE PRESIDENT IN HAITI

Sometimes the most dangerous moments with CAT occurred before the mission began. I went to Haiti to do a CAT advance for Vice President Quayle. Haiti is the poorest country in the Western Hemisphere and one of the poorest in the world. Vice President Quayle's visit came in the midst of a great deal of political unrest.

From the moment of the advance team's arrival, the situation was tense. The CAT advance team traveled in an Air Force C-141. We landed at the Port-au-Prince airport, a spot straight out of a bad movie. The median along the one runway was littered with the wreckages of several derelict DC-3s. The terminal building was a bullet-pockmarked reminder of periods of unrest.

Upon the team's arrival, the Department of State Regional Security Officer (RSO) briefed us. He told us that over the past few days some policemen had been captured and burned alive by the criminal element of the local population. The criminals would corner the police officer and get him to use all his ammunition. Then they would place a tire over his head, pinning his arms to his side. Next they filled the tire with gasoline and lit it. I had come to a menacing time and place.

I traveled with a Sig Sauer P226 9mm pistol along with 5 magazines of 15 rounds each and an M16 rifle with 180 rounds of ammunition. After the RSO's briefing, I carried both. In addition to telling us about the human torches, the RSO stated firmly that we should never, *under any circumstances,* step outside our vehicle in Port-au-Prince. If our vehicle broke down, we were to immediately contact the embassy and request assistance.

During this unrest, it was thought that any American caught on the streets would receive the same treatment as the local police. I decided not to be taken alive, if cornered. I was determined to take as many attackers as possible with me before ending the episode on my own terms.

Each morning the advance team got into an armored Suburban for the drive from the hotel to the embassy. We went straight through downtown Port-au-Prince. Anytime we slowed, locals surrounded our vehicle. I sat in the right front seat with my rifle, hoping the old Suburban would make it safely to the embassy yet again. Each morning we saw at least one dead body lying somewhere near the embassy or floating in the ocean.

Another threat came in the form of malaria-carrying mosquitoes. We had to be aware of all threats, insect, human, or otherwise. With the buzz of mosquitoes and the "crack" of nearby gunfire, I slept lightly with a sheet wrapped to my neck—to deter the mosquitoes—and my Sig Sauer gripped in my right hand.

One night we did not sleep at all. A particularly dangerous part of our advance work included a night move from the embassy to the airport, then back to the embassy. We were to meet the air force cargo plane carrying the VP's armored vehicles, additional agents, and my own CAT team. Haiti was a land without law at that time. CAT was the only protection we could count on if we were ambushed. We made it through that long night with no incidents.

On the day the VP was to land in Haiti, we waited apprehensively. Since our arrival, we had seen few if any police or military. Now, large numbers of Haitian militia surrounded the airport and paced along the tarmac armed with M1 Garand rifles. As I wandered over to look at the soldiers and their weapons, I noticed that some ammunition clipped to rifle slings was black-tipped—indicating armor-piercing capability. Seeing so many Haitians armed with rifles that had an effective range of over five hundred yards and ammunition that could punch through armor was of grave concern.

Days before the VP came to Haiti, we had negotiated the details of his protection with the local authorities. This "force" was not a part of our agreed upon plan. We were told the soldiers added to the protection of the VP. This did not ease our apprehension. All eyes turned to the airstrip as Air Force Two landed and taxied to the terminal. The CAT Suburban slowly moved into position to best observe, and if necessary, neutralize the Haitian militia.

Sometimes a decent *show* of force is as good as the *use* of force. The unwanted militia behaved themselves in a quiet, docile manner, seemingly afraid to handle their rifles or even to look at us. We maintained control of the situation throughout the VP's visit.

After the VP's departure, we left on an old C-141 that appeared somewhat questionable as to its airworthiness. However, we were all willing to take a chance on this plane rather than stay in Haiti one more night. We boarded the plane, which had been sitting in the sun for over an hour. The interior temperature was over 110 degrees!

As we took our seats in the stifling heat, the pilot announced, "There is no water on board. I understand that many of you are carrying a small supply of water. Would you be willing to share whatever you have by pouring it into the cooler up front?" Not enough water in that heat was a serious situation.

No one hesitated. We quickly formed a line to pour whatever water remained in our personal containers into the communal supply. As a result of this sharing, everyone had enough water for the trip back to DC. This is one of the things about Secret Service agents. An agent might try to steal your date, but he would give you his last dollar, his last beer, or the last of his water merely for the asking.

THE COUNTER ASSAULT TEAM OLYMPICS

As one might imagine, most Secret Service agents are highly aggressive personalities, both men and women. In CAT, ALL agents are highly aggressive and competitive. CAT agents are "beyond" highly competitive, just like athletes on sports teams. Like a football team, we might have disagreements that come close to blows, but we of CAT were brothers, colleagues, and teammates. We would do nearly anything for one another, from loaning money with no worry of repayment, to taking another agent's midnight shift so he could stay home with his sick wife or child, or even sharing our last bit of food or water on a foreign trip in inhospitable areas. We also would do practically *anything* to beat each other at absolutely everything we did. No life's event was out of range for our competiveness. In CAT, one was either first or last with nothing in the middle.

For example, if an agent fired a near perfect score on the range with the M16 rifle and Sig Pistol, everyone else intensified their efforts to beat that agent, even if by only one point. Being good was never good enough. Everyone wanted to be the best. The monthly physical fitness test became a spectacle worthy of the Roman Coliseum minus the lions. Each agent would risk permanent injury in order to be the best in pull-ups or the 1.5-mile run. Immediate action drills with more than one team sometimes produced injuries. Teams tried to outdo the other in terms of speed in exiting the CAT vehicle and closing on the enemy instructors. Like an attack dog that has to be pulled off a handler pretending to be a bad guy, teams sometimes had to be pulled off instructors as the team overran the instructors' position in a mock attack. Sometimes when no physical outlet was readily available, interactions in the truck and on the road could become tense between these competitive personalities. The worst of these situations occurred when there was little travel and teams had too much down time (or too much truck time). Such days meant five or six CAT agents sitting caged in a Suburban for up to twelve hours while waiting for an attack on the president (that thankfully seldom came). In order to alleviate pent-up energy and aggression, the special agents in charge came up with an idea for the annual CAT Olympics.

All CAT agents participated in three events: 1) maximum bench press; 2) 1.5-mile run; and 3) weapons scores. Recognition would be given to the top five individuals. Teams would be rated one through six. We were given a month to train before the competition. Each agent immersed completely in a training regimen. Everyone had his own master plan of increasing bench press and decreasing run time.

When competition began, it was indeed an Olympics. Everyone participated in each event with dead seriousness and complete focus. CAT physical training records were bested time and again. Everyone wanted to be first. Certainly no one wanted to be last.

Some agents literally passed out at the end of the run. More than one barbell had to be lifted off an agent who had maxed out his dynamic strength. Everyone had a lot of fun competing directly with every other agent to be Top CAT and a member of the Top Team. When it was over, our boss read the final results. I was very surprised that I placed third out of thirty-six agents. It wasn't first, but considering the caliber of competition and being a CAT rookie, I was pleased.

The first place team received a trophy, as did the last place team. Yes, last place did receive a trophy. The last place team award for the first CAT Olympics was a miniature bronze toilet seat with a spent M16 shell casing inside.

★ 6 ★

From CAT to PPD

TRAINING FOR THE WORST

In order to maintain our highest level of readiness, we trained constantly. When not protecting POTUS, we ran immediate action drills, practiced on the firing range, or worked out in the gym. As good as we were at our work, we got better after a new agent was placed in charge of CAT training. A former Navy SEAL, he took CAT training to new heights and set a standard that continues to this day.

Through this new training, our skills became even sharper. There was one problem with the training, and it was potentially lethal. CAT protected POTUS, as did the PPD working shift, but the two details seldom trained together.

In the event of an attack on POTUS, PPD shift agents and CAT agents did not know what the other group would do—beyond, of course, covering and evacuating POTUS. To remedy this shortcoming, CAT and the PPD shift began regularly training together. Problems quickly surfaced that now could be corrected.

One of the first joint training exercises took place at Kennebunkport, Maine, at the Bush compound. President George H. W. Bush agreed to allow the Secret Service full access to the compound for some realistic practice.

The first drill required CAT to respond to the main house, "kill" attackers, and consolidate its positions around the house. Within seconds of securing the residence, a PPD agent ran around the corner of the house. He promptly "shot" me with his blank-filled training weapon. The bizarre thing is that this agent and I knew each other. I had a label in large letters on my back: POLICE. In the excitement over the attack, he developed tunnel vision. When he saw a man in a black outfit, he simply blasted him with an Uzi.

The problem is not unique. Under stress, even in

training, some people can totally lose the ability to think clearly. All situational awareness goes out the window. As a result, the confused person can shoot someone known to him because all he sees is a black uniform and a rifle. These drills were invaluable in helping CAT and the PPD shift work together as a harmonious unit. The exercises also alerted us to the fact that certain agents had to be watched more closely during times of stress.

THE BOLDNESS OF THE PRESIDENCY

Many of our presidents, including John F. Kennedy and George H. W. Bush, have documented histories of physical courage during military service. As commander in chief of the armed forces, POTUS presides over the boldest group of men and women in the world, our men and women in uniform. Some presidents occasionally want to be seen, in the eyes of these warriors, as men of courage, not just suits wearing expensive watches. They desire to be viewed as equals in nerve and boldness.

One example of the type of man who becomes president is John F. Kennedy. He commanded a PT boat in the South Pacific during World War II. PT boats, only eighty feet long, were built mostly of plywood for speed and maneuverability. These small boats raced about creating havoc and fighting the much larger Japanese destroyers. Propelled by two enormous General Motors engines that dined on flammable high octane aviation fuel, PT boats made a huge explosion if hit by enemy guns.

After losing his first boat, PT-109, and recovering from his injuries, Kennedy rejected going home to safety and the celebrity of a returning hero. Instead, he requested the command of another PT boat and served to do battle with Japanese forces again.

JFK was driven by his desire to serve America and his love of adventure. Before the war, Kennedy was not interested in politics. When his older brother, Joe Jr., a naval aviator, was killed in action, John's father worked to make John a popular politician. After becoming president, JFK took excessive risks from time to time. The most notable examples came in the way he immersed himself in large crowds of people where anyone could have killed him.

Perhaps President Kennedy thought surviving World War II and being the youngest person elected to the presidency made him invincible. He was not.

Another president no stranger to risk was President George H. W. Bush. A World War II naval aviator, Bush flew low-level bombing missions against

Agent Clint Hill shielding President and Mrs. Kennedy seconds after the assassination. (*Public domain*)

Running is a big part of agent training. Here I am with a class running the perimeter of the training academy. (*Personal collection of Dan Emmett*)

Pugil stick training to simulate bayonet fighting. (*Photo by Corporal Jess Levens, USMC*)

As a first lieutenant home on leave, December 1979. (*Personal collection of Dan Emmett*)

Climbing rope with a class on the obstacle course. (*Personal collection of Dan Emmett*)

With Senator Kennedy at Hyannis Port, Massachusetts, on Election Day, 1984. (*Personal collection of Dan Emmett*)

The Bridge of No Return, looking into North Korea. The Communist observation post is visible in the upper left-hand corner of the bridge. (*Personal collection of Dan Emmett*)

My CAT team in Korea preparing to move to the Bridge of No Return. (Left to right: Agents Charlie White, Jim Cobb, Mike Carbone, the author, and agent Lee Fields.) That is North Korea behind the line. (*Personal collection of Dan Emmett*)

Donnelle and I with President and Mrs. Bush at the White House Christmas party 1992. (*Photo courtesy of The White House*)

With President Bill Clinton in Georgetown, 1993. President Clinton loved large crowds; the larger the better. That is me on the far right wearing the game face. We had just emerged from the Sequoia restaurant in Georgetown on a Sunday morning into a large crowd and had been in one place far too long. (*Photo courtesy of The White House*)

Keeping an eye
on things with
President Clinton
in the pressroom at
the White House.
(*Photo courtesy of
The White House*)

Donnelle and I with President Clinton at the White House
Christmas party, 1994. (*Photo courtesy of The White House*)

All presidents I
protected were
always cordial to
their agents and
families. Here, my
son and I say hello
to President Clinton
in the Oval Office.
(*Photo courtesy of The
White House*)

From inside a CAT truck following Air Force One, tail number 27000, with President George Herbert Walker Bush inside. Note the crack in the windshield from a previous encounter with this jet. Although the engine thrust was less with this airplane than the larger 747, it was still formidable. Damaged windshields were not uncommon from following too closely. (*Personal collection of Dan Emmett*)

Marine One departs the White House. (*Photo courtesy of The White House*)

President Clinton and I leaving the White House for a run through downtown Washington, DC, where anyone could be waiting with a gun. (*Photo courtesy of The White House*)

A 1993 Cadillac armored limousine first used by President Clinton. This vehicle sported a 450-cubic-inch engine. Although long retired from service, the actual weight remains classified. (*Photo courtesy of The White House*)

SATC 138 at Fort Meade obstacle course, 1995. I am at the far left. John Mrha is at the far right. (*Personal collection of Dan Emmett*)

With President Bush in the Oval Office. (*Photo courtesy of The White House*)

Leaving the White House as an agent for the last time. (*Personal collection of Dan Emmett*)

Japanese targets in a Grumman Avenger off the deck of a small aircraft carrier. Awarded the Distinguished Flying Cross for his skill and courage under fire, he parachuted into the Pacific Ocean after his bomber was struck by ground fire. The life raft in which he floated while awaiting rescue drifted very close to the Japanese-occupied island of Chichijima he had just bombed.

Fortunately, the American submarine, *Finback,* plucked the future president from the sea, saving him from a cruel fate. Lieutenant Bush then became an "accidental" submariner until the *Finback* could deliver him back to his carrier.

President Bush never quite got over his love of physical danger, as demonstrated by his numerous parachute jumps since leaving office. Even though he was a former president, he was still protected by the Secret Service. During these parachute jumps, his Secret Service detail could do little more than wait on the ground hoping the former president's parachute would not fail.

I am often asked, "Who has the final say regarding the president's activities—the president or the Secret Service?" The answer is both, with the president having by far the most control.

For example, the Secret Service may discourage

the president from engaging in dangerous acts such as landing on a carrier in a jet or shaking hands with people who have not been screened for weapons. The Secret Service will not openly defy the president's wishes. However, the Secret Service should remove—by force, if necessary—a president who wishes to shake hands with a group known to harbor a hostile gunman. In other words, barring specific knowledge of tangible, imminent danger, the president usually does what he wishes to do, while the Secret Service does its best to protect him.

President Bush's boldness became apparent when he insisted on a visit to Los Angeles, California, in the wake of riots following the Rodney King verdict. Police in L.A. had beaten a man named Rodney King following a high-speed pursuit and King's resisting arrest. Bystanders videoed the moment. Riots broke out in South Central L.A. when a court acquitted the police of any wrongdoing.

Mobs took to the streets destroying cars, burning buildings, smashing windows, stealing goods from stores, shooting guns, and acting lawlessly. President Bush decided to go to L.A. to see for himself what had happened and hopefully to calm down the situation. While the Secret Service was against this idea, President Bush was insistent, and so we went.

This motorcade was different from most others in that we had the deputy director of the Secret Service in my CAT vehicle.

I had been given the choice of either him in my truck, or the director of the Secret Service. This was my wish, because the son of the director was a member of my team and I did not want father and son to be together in this situation. I feared the director might in a crisis instinctively give orders to his son that could be in direct conflict with my own. Our team formed up behind a hangar at LAX to begin "gearing up" and briefing. I was aware that our extra team member (aka the deputy director of the Secret Service) was standing off to the side away from our gathering. I thought he was probably as uncomfortable with the situation as we were.

When he made no move to join the team, it became clear that I as team leader had to brief the deputy director. He did not seem to know what to do next. I walked the twenty feet across the hangar apron, introduced myself, and welcomed him to our team. We then walked to the truck where I introduced the deputy director to each team member. I briefed him on what I expected of him should we come under fire and be forced to respond. While he was the Number Two Man in the Secret Service, his authority ended at my truck. I was the team leader. We would proceed tactically as if he were simply not there.

My counterpart on the other team had drawn the Number One Man in the Secret Service for his truck. He decided to place him in the backseat facing forward. I, on the other hand, placed my new cargo in the well of the Suburban facing to the rear with the "base of fire" agent facing backward. In this position, he would not be in the way of the maneuver element should the team deploy. My instructions to him were simple: "Sir, if we deploy, remain with the vehicle and provide rear security for the base of fire agent."

He seemed fine with this, which made things easier. The last thing I needed was to enter into a discussion with the deputy over seating. While I understood the desire of the director and the deputy director to be in the motorcade, we all wished they had chosen another place to ride rather than with us.

We boarded the truck with our visitor in the well. POTUS arrived via Air Force One and entered the limousine for the trip downtown. The motorcade from LAX to South Central L.A. was tense. We were told by the Los Angeles Police Department to expect sniper fire. We could clearly see people on tops of buildings and inside open windows. We received no hostile fire, at least that we were aware of. POTUS was inside an armored vehicle, so we had no real concerns about his safety even if we did take fire. That level of concern changed when we got to the affected neighborhood.

Upon arriving in South Central L.A. and the riot area, POTUS ordered the limo to stop. Then to our great concern—and contrary to the itinerary—he got out. He walked down the sidewalk among still smoldering debris, inspecting storefronts with broken-out windows. We felt this was very unwise as many owners guarded their buildings with a large assortment of shoulder weapons and handguns to protect them against further damage from rioters. Not sure of their mood or intent, we watched them closely, ready to eliminate attackers if necessary.

Our task was to protect POTUS in this unusual situation within our own country. There was no traffic or cheering crowd. The president, his staff, and his PPD walked in the open in the midst of a difficult time in America. This was a tense moment fraught with danger, but one that displayed President Bush's courage and leadership.

TO KOREA AGAIN

My Counter Assault Team (CAT) accompanied President Bill Clinton's PPD to South Korea in 1993. This was my second trip to the Asian nation. Even though the Korean War was fought before I was born, I knew its history. In June 1950, Communist forces from North Korea invaded the south and attempted to unify the Korean peninsula under one government—a Communist one.

After three years of fighting, the war stopped with a cease-fire agreement. There was no surrender or peace treaty, only an agreement to not shoot at each other. Technically, a state of war still exists to this day between North and South Korea. The cease-fire established an area that neither side could control, called the Demilitarized Zone (DMZ). The DMZ runs across the Korean peninsula roughly along the 38th north parallel of latitude for about 150 miles and is 2.4 miles wide (1.2 miles on each side of the cease-fire line). Both countries have heavily fortified their side of the DMZ.

As anyone who watches the news knows, North Korea can be extremely unpredictable and capable of aggressive talk and unprovoked deadly aggression. It has been deemed best not to unnecessarily provoke North Korea. Yet, in spite of this volatility, President Clinton, or someone on his staff, decided the president should do a photo op on the Bridge of No Return.

This bridge runs through the cease-fire line (38th parallel north) from one country to the other. It was across this bridge that American Prisoners of War (POWs) walked to freedom in 1953 when North Korea chose to release them. Since the cease-fire agreement in 1953, North Korea has controlled the northern end of the bridge and South Korea the southern end. On the northern side, an observation post occupies high ground, providing a perfect view of any activities on the bridge.

Near the south end of the bridge is a United Nations observation post, which was the site of unprovoked violence by the always-unpredictable North Korean troops. In 1976, ax-wielding North Korean soldiers murdered two US Army officers, Captain Art Bonifas and First Lieutenant Mark Barrett. Seventeen years later, this area where the murders occurred would be the arrival point for President Clinton's motorcade.

As part of the cease-fire arrangements, no rifles were allowed in this area. Also, the closest significant American forces were outside the DMZ—over one mile away. Even with this agreement, PPD directed CAT to get into position at the end of the bridge. We were to be armed only with pistols so we could monitor POTUS, the bridge, and the North Korean observation post. I applied my own definition to the word *monitor.*

The United States informed North Korea ahead of time that POTUS would be coming to the bridge. This was a diplomatic as well as smart decision. The Communists would have gone ballistic over the sight of President Clinton and company on the bridge unannounced.

The night before the president's visit to the bridge, the commanding officer of Camp Bonifas (named for the deceased officer), hosted all the Secret Service personnel on the trip for a dinner at the officers' club. The colonel, a veteran of both Vietnam and Desert Storm, described the situation in black-and-white terms.

"If attacked and you survive the assault, and chances are you will not, you will be only a speed bump for the North Korean army," he said grimly. "We have a squad of shock troops waiting just outside the DMZ who will immediately ride to battle. But . . . they are ten minutes away. In any case, it will be the longest ten minutes of your life. . . ."

All on the team appreciated his honest appraisal. We gladly accepted this warrior's toast to our success and to the survival of the team and the president.

The next day, my team geared up and mounted our Humvee for the move to the Bridge of No Return. We had only rolled a few yards when the voice of the command post agent (and CAT schoolmate of mine and as of this writing, the director of the United States Secret Service), Joe Clancy, jolted me with its urgency. Joe's voice was usually calmer than calm. On this occasion, strain accented his words. From Joe's voice I knew something was wrong and what it probably was.

"Hawkeye from command post," Joe forcefully broadcasted over the encrypted frequency.

"Damn Joe," I thought to myself, lowering the volume on the radio. "CP from Hawkeye, go ahead," I answered.

"Hawkeye from CP," Joe responded. "Be advised that numerous North Korean soldiers have been observed moving into the northern sector of the bridge armed with AK-47 rifles."

I turned and gave my team an "I told you so" look. I keyed my microphone and simply replied, "CP from Hawkeye, roger that."

I had anticipated this entirely predictable event

well in advance. Never had I intended letting my team go to the bridge armed only with pistols. Before we left Camp Bonifas, I ordered the team to carry the full complement of arms and ammunition— pistols, M16s, and over one thousand rounds of ammunition. I was prepared to assume full responsibility for that decision.

In addition, I had ordered team members to carry their rifles with a round in the chamber, violating a major Secret Service regulation for long guns. Since we were not supposed to have our M16s to begin with, the round-in-the-chamber regulation seemed a minor violation. Given how outnumbered we were, the extra second it took to chamber a round under fire might be the difference of POTUS or the team surviving an ambush.

The situation was serious—damned serious, in fact. I was not willing to risk my team or the life of the president based on a forty-year-old agreement. I had correctly predicted the Communists would break the agreement and now we were ready. Because the North Koreans expected Americans to always play by the rules, the Communists did not expect us to have rifles. This incorrect assumption tilted the odds slightly more in our favor.

We continued on to the Bridge of No Return

with this new knowledge. At the bridge, we found the Communists in and around their observation post arrogantly brandishing their Kalashnikov AK-47 rifles. To the Secret Service, the only reason North Koreans would violate the no-rifle agreement was because shooting the president of the United States is much easier with rifles than with their Russian-provided Makarov pistols.

The terrain around the bridge was a combination of dirt and asphalt road surrounded by fields and forests. The area was heavily mined. Even a small deviation off the road would produce a big, flaming "kaboom." So, we moved carefully. We picked the best deployment position for an attack. It was not directly at the arrival point but near enough to respond by fire and maneuver. The North Koreans were watching us with binoculars and pointing riflescopes at us.

We counter-eyed them with our own binoculars. However, even though our M16s were scoped, we kept our rifles out of sight. Unlike our North Korean nemesis, we at least concealed our weapons, giving no indication that we were violating the apparently meaningless clause in the 1953 cease-fire agreement.

The North Koreans we now faced were the sons and

grandsons of men who killed thousands of Americans from 1950 to 1953. From birth, each of the soldiers on the opposite end of the bridge had been taught to hate America, its form of government, and its leaders. They thought resuming the war with the United States was both inevitable and desirable. The shooting part of the Korean War ended in 1953 with a truce, but technically we were still at war. If they wanted to resume the shooting war again, that day would have been a perfect day.

Our mission to fight a delaying action while POTUS escaped was pretty much certain death should things break bad. The commander of the area had warned us the night before. We did not doubt that in addition to the soldiers in the observation post armed with AK-47s only yards from where POTUS would be standing, there were probably more in the tall grass on the other side of the bridge.

This scenario is exactly why CAT exists and why CAT training is so intense. With only a one-word command from me, the team would be out of the vehicle and directing a heavy volume of pinpoint accurate fire on the objective in less than four seconds. Regardless of our own fate in the seconds that would follow, the hope was that we would accomplish our mission and POTUS would live another day.

Everyone on my team knew this truth. We accepted our job with no complaints. We had no intention of being mere sacrificial lambs or dying a glorious death. However, we were confident that the five of us would produce many, many dead Communists if they decided to do something as ill-advised as trying to kill an American president.

The mood in the CAT vehicle was serious, quiet, and confident as I announced our plan of action in the event of an attack. Each man indicated with a grim smile that he understood his assignment. I had total confidence that each would do his duty and respond per his training. We were brothers in arms who worked together, trained together, and traveled the world together. Now, if necessary, we would meet our fates together. We all shook hands and waited for the arrival of POTUS at what was nothing less than a made-to-order kill zone. It was time to earn our pay.

At the designated time, President Clinton and his PPD shift arrived at the bridge. As POTUS emerged from the right rear seat, he was immediately surrounded by the shift. From our position, we could see a noticeable increase in activity and movement from the North Korean observation post. If a gunfight were going to happen, it would be within the next few seconds.

I felt calm yet hyper-alert as adrenaline kicked in. I could feel my heart rate increase as my grip tightened on the hand guard of my rifle still concealed beneath the instrument panel of the Humvee. We scanned the surrounding area and stared at the North Koreans who in turn stared back. Meanwhile, President Clinton leisurely strolled along the Bridge of No Return as if he were at Camp David. He appeared satisfied and relaxed, a man with no concerns.

After walking a little farther onto the bridge than he probably should have, practically over the line into North Korea, President Clinton looked around the area. He simply stood there for a few minutes and then returned to his vehicle. We got the hell out of the zone.

NEXT ASSIGNMENT: PPD WORKING SHIFT

I loved my assignment in CAT. It was the best four years of my career. Four years is a long time, though, and I was ready to move on. One day, after the trip to South Korea with President Clinton, I was called to the PPD office. The assistant special agent in charge said, "Dan, your time is up in CAT. Where do you want to go next? You can have almost any assignment you want in the Secret Service."

Without hesitation, I replied, "I want to stay on PPD and become a member of the working shift."

"Okay," he replied with a smile. "Report for duty on Monday."

For me, this was as euphoric as my initial selection as a Secret Service agent ten years earlier. Just as the selection process to become an agent is long, so, too, is the one to become an agent on the PPD shift. For me, the process lasted ten years.

In those years with the Secret Service, I had attained all of my major career goals. Through planning, tenacity, and a little luck, I had managed to land the prime assignments sought after by most young agents but realized by few. I had joined the ranks of such notable agents as Clint Hill, Jerry Parr, Tim McCarthy, and Larry Buendorf, as well as the thousands of anonymous agents who had directly protected POTUS since 1902. It was now my turn to safeguard the leader of the free world up close and personal. I was going to the White House.

On my first day as a PPD shift agent, I reported to the Secret Service command post in the West Wing for the daily briefing five minutes early. I was always at least five minutes early. I found out that everyone else was ten minutes early. My shift leader introduced me to my shift mates and then briefed us for the day.

After the briefing, we moved from the West Wing to the main mansion, where I had worked many CAT midnight shifts for the past four years. We relieved the previous midnight shift and moved to our posts. The senior agent on the shift (called the shift "whip") walked me to each post, explaining the responsibilities. Although I had worked in the White House for four years as a CAT agent and even filled in as a shift agent, I did not know what the permanent shift responsibilities were or even the daily routine. I was the "new guy" who happened to know enough to move around the White House without getting lost, at least most of the time.

As a new agent on PPD, I had some tough moments learning the routine. Each day brought new challenges with what seemed a never-ending list of new things. Some items were written down. Others were not. A new agent received a set of small flash cards reminding him what his actions should be at each post. Also issued was a series of flash cards with diagrams of the various formations used in walking POTUS.

I had been on the shift about two weeks and learned just enough to be a menace. One morning while posted on the ground floor of the White House, the elevator light indicated that "Eagle" (the call sign for President Clinton) was on the way down. The elevator door opened and out came the president. According to standard operating procedure, I quietly announced over my sleeve microphone, "Eagle moving to the Oval."

Off we went, with me leading POTUS to his office for another day of whatever presidents do. Of course, he did not need to be led. But there always had to be an agent close.

All was routine. As we reached the Oval Office, I opened the colonnade door with Eagle close behind. As we entered, I did a quick look-see to make sure all was in order. Then I exited through what I thought was the door leading to the hallway between the Oval Office and the Roosevelt Room. It was not. I had mistakenly exited through the door leading into the private dining room of the Oval Office, which was next to the door I was supposed to use.

No one was in the dining room other than me. I stood there trying to decide what to do next. I should have taken another second or two to think, because I made the wrong decision. I turned and reentered the Oval Office to find a surprised and somewhat annoyed-looking President Clinton. I tried to look as though this were somehow planned, as I said, "Good morning, sir. All clear." I then exited through the correct door, leaving behind a puzzled POTUS.

As experienced as I was after ten years of working for the Secret Service, I still had plenty to learn as a member of the PPD working shift.

★ 7 ★

Running with the President

The Presidential Protection Division is the most important and prestigious division in the Secret Service. If an American president were to be assassinated, it would be a catastrophic event not only for the United States, but for the whole world as well. Failure is not an option for PPD. Nothing short of perfection is tolerated. The PPD stays within arm's length of the president and is the last line of defense to deter any attempt to harm the chief executive.

One frequently asked question of Secret Service agents is whether they are actually willing to take a bullet for the president. Most agents will change the subject or deflect the question with humor. For the record, the answer is yes. Few agents will publicly admit it. No one enjoys discussing it.

As an applicant to the Secret Service, I was told very early in the selection process that this was an expectation. If I was not willing to lay down my life for the president, I should apply for a job elsewhere. The subject never came up again in twenty-one years of service. It was simply understood.

For me personally, no one ever elected to the office of the presidency was worth dying for, yet the *office of the presidency* was. Presidents are people who live and breathe like anyone else, but the *office* of the presidency must be protected at all costs. Regardless of the president's party affiliation or an agent's personal feelings about the president, I respected and protected the role of chief executive.

A NEW PRESIDENT

President Bill Clinton was the first president I guarded as a PPD working shift agent. When Clinton moved into the White House, the Secret Service learned to work with another new administration. Clinton was the seventeenth president the Secret Service would protect. Every presidential staff has its own way of working and scheduling for POTUS. The Secret

Service is rigid in its mission and discipline, but has to remain flexible regarding the desires of the president and the demands of individual situations.

ON FOOT

President Clinton regularly ran around the open, unsecured streets of Washington, DC, and the world. Agents who ran with President Clinton performed one of the most dangerous assignments possible. In, this case, the question would be: "Would you take a bullet, a speeding car, or a city bus for the president?"

During Clinton's campaign, he developed the habit of running as a form of exercise and a way to meet voters. The best way to do this as a candidate was to run in public places. His running presented a large and unusual security challenge to the Secret Service.

To properly protect candidate Clinton during these runs required at least one or two agents to run alongside him. These agents had to run with their weapon and communication gear. At first it was no problem keeping up with Clinton. As time progressed, he lost weight and became more fit. He also began running farther and faster. Soon, the Service had to find agents who were in good enough shape to run with him.

When Clinton became president, he decided to

keep his early morning runs. This meant that agents had to run with the president for three to four miles bearing the weight of a gun and radio. Clinton insisted on running in broad daylight on the streets of DC instead of within the confines of the White House grounds. (President Harry Truman, who loved to make rapid walks, once described the White House grounds as "a prison.")

There is always a degree of risk with any trip, even when the president is encased in an armored vehicle. Clinton's runs were deadly serious. POTUS was regularly running the "mean" and always potentially dangerous streets of Washington during morning rush hour. Anyone could stand within a few feet of the president as he ran by.

Taking the president running at peak rush hour down Pennsylvania Avenue, around the Reflecting Pool at the Lincoln Memorial, or through Rock Creek Park, bordered on insanity. The most dangerous part of the morning run was its predictability. Anyone could be lying in ambush.

On a run, all of the equipment designed to protect the president—metal detectors, K9 explosives-detecting dogs, CAT, ballistic shields, armored vehicles—were useless. The Service tried to convince the president to run on a track within the White

House grounds or at a nearby military base. But part of the reason Clinton wanted to run was to be out among people and away from the White House.

The Service utilized CAT and extra agents to surround the president and then hoped for the best. Also, the president himself provided an odd source of assistance by inviting friends and supporters to run with him. These extra people unknowingly presented excellent ballistic insulation.

There was never an uneventful run with President Clinton. On almost every outing there was an incident of some sort. A public-running POTUS was not a good idea. It was unsafe for him as well as the public.

One particularly memorable run began at the Reflecting Pool near the Lincoln Memorial. The first incident happened even before the run began. A motorist, amazed to see the president of the United States in running apparel, stared at POTUS until he rear-ended the car in front of him.

After that, the run began normally. POTUS moved at his usual nine- to ten-minute-per-mile pace around the Reflecting Pool. Suddenly, to the surprise and horror of his agents, POTUS crossed Seventeenth Street without the benefit of a crosswalk. He ran up the gradual but increasingly steep incline toward the Washington Monument and *lots* of tourists. This was definitely NOT the usual routine of two or three times around the Reflecting Pool and then home to the White House.

I was one of two agents running a short distance behind the president. As POTUS ascended the hill toward the monument, the supervisor beside the president began to slow. The supervisor then signaled for me to take the off-shoulder position with POTUS. I sprinted uphill a good seventy-five yards to close the distance between me and POTUS who seemed unconcerned that he was without agent coverage.

I zipped past the supervisor with reserve energy born of adrenaline, desperately trying to catch POTUS before he topped the hill and disappeared from view. In my head I imagined Staff Sergeant McLean from my Quantico training days yelling, "You can rest after you are dead! Get to the top of the damn hill now!"

Just as POTUS reached the crest of the hill, I caught up with him. We now faced thirty stunned tourists at the base of the Washington Monument. Each began scrambling for what I hoped were cameras as I moved between them and POTUS. My right hand went inside my jacket and found the grip of my pistol. We descended the hill with me looking over my shoulder at the tourists. No other agent was in sight.

Moments later, President Clinton said, "Okay, Dan, let's go home."

"Yes, sir," I answered, trying to sound less out of breath than I actually was. We reversed course and headed back up toward the waiting tourists now aiming their cameras at POTUS. My biggest concern now was that he would stop and work the crowd. He merely waved, however, and continued down the side of the hill back to Seventeenth and the waiting cars.

At the motorcade, the president performed his usual stretching exercises next to the limo. This was the most dangerous time of the run—our presence was well known because we had been in the general area for thirty-five minutes. The police had just finished working the accident that occurred at the beginning of the run. Traffic was backed up. Many people converged on the area as the president finally got back into the limo. This scenario was the norm three to four days per week.

The biggest problem with President Clinton's fitness program was that he ran in areas where any assassin could lurk. He (and we) ran through crowds and crossed city streets. We stood in the open by the limo for minutes at a time while the president stretched before and after the run. All of this happened with normal traffic flowing by.

We also violated one of the most basic rules for security. We usually left the White House at the same time each day, used the same gate, and seldom varied our running sites or routes. We had four running venues and did not mix them up very well. We were an assassination waiting to happen. Were it not for a well-timed overseas trip, an attempted assassination could have had dire results.

During December 1993, President Clinton left Washington for a two-week trip to Russia. Meanwhile, a man in Florida was plotting to kill the president. His basic plan was to drive from Orlando to Washington, where he would wait on a park bench along one of our running routes. When President Clinton ran by, the man was going to kill him. Theorists believe the attacker wished to die in a hail of Secret Service pistol lead.

The Secret Service has always benefited from the fact that most potential assassins are largely unable to make and implement effective plans. Fortunately, this man's plans were no different. The place where he sat day after day for over a week was indeed on a route we used regularly. In this instance, the would-be assassin failed to realize that POTUS was out of the country. Thus, the president would not be running by that park bench anytime soon.

The would-be assassin eventually grew tired of waiting in the cold and returned to sunny Florida. At home, he confided what he had done to a friend, who contacted authorities. The suspect was arrested and convicted for threatening the life of a president. He served four years in a federal prison.

As a result of this incident and others not publicly revealed, the Service finally convinced President Clinton to stop the unwise practice of running in public. The president had pushed his luck long enough and gotten away with it. Everyone knew his luck would not hold forever.

AIR FORCE ONE

In an agent's career there are certain moments that will always stand out and be remembered forever. One of the most awe-inspiring events for me was flying on Air Force One for the first time. Flying on AF-1 was always special for many reasons. Nothing symbolizes the power and prestige of the presidency and the United States more than this magnificent aircraft. Very few Secret Service agents flew on AF-1— only those assigned to PPD.

My first flight on Air Force One occurred one night during the summer of 1993. My shift and I began this adventure with a drive from the White House to an off-site landing zone.

As we climbed the steps into the HMX-1 helicopter, a marine sergeant in full dress blues saluted. The salute was a standard courtesy rendered by the marine aircrew for all who flew on their helicopter.

As a former marine officer, I instinctively returned the squared-away sergeant's salute. It was not a part of protocol. But protocol or not, as a former marine officer, it was a habit I would never break.

The helicopter rose into the purple night sky and circled slowly over Washington. We waited for Marine One to lift off from the White House and then flew in formation to Andrews Air Force Base. When we arrived, the president exited Marine One to a crisp marine salute. He then walked over to Air Force One and ascended the front stairway.

The Secret Service PPD shift boarded the rear stairway to the aircraft. An Air Force sergeant checks the names of all who board AF-1. Up the stairs I went to the Secret Service compartment, located toward the rear of the plane. It was just forward of the White House Traveling Press Corps' compartment.

As I prepared for my first flight on Air Force One, I took my coat off and hung it in a closet next to our lavatory. I kept my gun and radio. Even though we were on AF-1, we were still working and expected to respond to any crisis. Technically, we were at the White House in the air. We worked and behaved as if we were on duty at the White House in Washington.

While I settled in, an air force enlisted person came by and cheerfully offered sodas, coffee, and snacks. Later I learned that, if it was mealtime, they also brought sandwiches that always tasted better than anything from the best restaurants. This great service was particularly welcome after a long day out with POTUS. We would often arrive at the plane exhausted and a bit stressed from a long day of keeping the leader of the free world alive. As soon as we took off our coats, the air force steward was there with drinks, snacks, lunch, or dinner. Even with movies and snacks, the Secret Service agents remained on duty. You never really relaxed.

On that first flight, as we sat watching a movie and enjoying a Coke, I saw President Clinton standing in our section. He then moved into the press compartment to conduct an impromptu media session. After the president answered a few questions from the traveling press, he came back into our compartment. He stopped briefly to offer some friendly words to our shift before returning to his compartment.

When the sound of the engines lessened, the

plane's nose dropped. We had begun our descent. This was our signal to start getting ready. The pilot got the plane on the ground as quickly as possible and on this, my first flight; I was still putting on my jacket when the main landing gear hit the runway. It was dark, and I was a bit startled when we landed, not realizing how close we were to the ground.

The entire shift was up and walking around while the pilot braked and reversed thrusters. We bounced and staggered as if we were on a rough section of train track. The plane no sooner braked to a halt than the rear door opened. We ran down the stairs and out into the waiting night to protect the president of the United States. I had completed my first of many rides on Air Force One as a full-fledged member of a working shift of the Presidential Protection Division.

FOREIGN TRAVEL

Foreign travel can be interesting and exciting. However, if you are a PPD agent, it means working long hours with jet lag and sleep deprivation. Too often it involves trying to keep your nutrition level to a point where you can function. Due to changing time zones, biorhythms get totally out of phase. Sometimes regularity habits kick in at the worst possible moments.

On one trip to Europe, I was preposted to a large ballroom where POTUS was to have a meeting. The hotel was an old and ornate building with high ceilings and priceless artwork—very European.

As I waited for POTUS, my internal mechanisms began to rumble. This was trouble on a large scale. I needed to find a men's room, or even a ladies' room. For the first and only time in my Secret Service career, I abandoned my post. I fled to a men's room across the hall from the room where POTUS was to arrive any minute. The odds that an assassin would appear in the next two minutes were nearly zero. However, the certainty that I *had* to find a restroom was 100 percent!

I rushed into the ornate men's room and found a beautiful stall. Two minutes later, I quickly reassembled equipment and myself. I ran to the door to return to my post. I flung it open and literally ran into the president of the United States, William Jefferson Clinton, almost knocking him down.

It seemed his internal clock was still on Washington time, the same as mine. As I moved aside to allow him entry, I blurted out in my most professional voice, "All clear, sir."

"Thanks, Dan," he said as he entered to tend to his presidential business.

My shift leader nodded to me and we left the

leader of the free world alone in his now private bathroom. As I moved back to my post, it occurred to me that the shift leader thought I was checking the men's room for POTUS. It was too perfect. I let him continue to think that forever.

I quickly learned that foreign trips were seldom exotic or exciting. We could be in one of the most beautiful cities in the world and never really see the place. During one trip to Budapest I worked the afternoon to midnight shift. It was dark when we arrived, and we never left the hotel during my shift. We could have been in Cleveland, Ohio, for all I knew.

The saying in the Service was that no matter where you go, once you arrive, there you are. Generally speaking that summed up foreign travel for me. Even though I never fully got to enjoy locations, I experienced many of the world's cultures and sights. From Jerusalem to Moscow, from London to Manila, from Korea to Syria, and many points in between, I traveled with the president of the United States.

In June 1994, I accompanied President Clinton to Europe for the fiftieth anniversary of D-Day. On this trip we visited the Normandy beaches where so many Americans died on June 6, 1945, to liberate France and all of Europe from Adolf Hitler and the Nazis. We also visited Cambridge, England, where thousands of monuments stood over empty graves for American airmen lost over Europe. One of the most noteworthy names we saw was Joseph P. Kennedy Jr. Young Joe Kennedy, older brother to JFK, had been killed on a mission to destroy German submarine pens in France. This trip reminded us the many sacrifices for freedom made by courageous Americans.

DRIVING THE PRESIDENT

After serving on the working shift for several months, I was moved to PPD's transportation section. There I would become one of a select few who drove POTUS in an armored limousine. During this assignment I would also drive the working shift in follow-up vehicles, and plan presidential motorcades. I was not a chauffeur, because in this new role I was charged with protecting the president as a highly trained agent.

The mission with the transportation section was twofold: 1) safely drive the president from Point A to Point B; and 2) do whatever is necessary to move the president out of a kill zone should the motorcade be attacked. For instance, it was the transportation section that rushed President Reagan to George Washington Hospital within minutes of his being shot in March 1981.

The presidential limousines were very large and very heavy. In spite of their 450-cubic-inch engines, there was a lag between stepping on the gas and the moment the car began to move. On the other hand, one had to begin braking well before the car was expected to stop. Some of the bulletproof glass caused a visual distortion.

Valentine's Day 1994 was a miserably cold, rain-soaked day in Washington. It was one of my first days in the transportation section. Nothing was on POTUS's schedule, so it looked to be a quiet evening. It did not turn out that way.

At around eight o'clock the phone rang. The shift leader announced that POTUS wanted to go to Andrews Air Force Base to surprise his wife, whose plane would arrive in two hours. I was to drive the limo. This should have been an easy assignment. I would simply be driving a car as big as a medium-sized boat with POTUS as my passenger. A limo I had yet to be fully checked out in.

The senior agent did the advance work while I readied the limo. We drove to the White House. While the senior agent met with his police counterpart, I sat alone. There in the belly of the beast I pondered the fact that I was to drive the president of the United States on a terribly rainy dark night in an off-the-record motorcade with no intersection control to surprise his wife on Valentine's Day. He obviously had a great deal of confidence in us.

The sound and movement of the door being opened broke my trance. In stepped the president and his daughter, Chelsea, with a simple, "Hi." President Clinton knew me from our runs and my time with him on the working shift. He knew most of his agents by name, due to his nearly photographic memory for faces.

"Good evening, Mr. President," I said and nodded at Chelsea. It now occurred to me that on the return trip, should we actually make it that far without rear-ending the lead vehicle, the First Lady would also be in the backseat. The detail leader settled into the front seat beside me. Over my earpiece, I heard the shift leader call the shift into the follow-up vehicle just behind us. The lead police car moved out and the detail leader looked at me and said, "Let's go." Off we went into the darkness and blinding rain.

The first obstacle to overcome was a serpentine course of barriers on the south grounds of the White House. Even with practice, of which I had none, I thought it impossible to avoid the damn things. Somehow I managed. The idea was not to jostle POTUS any more than was necessary. At the moment, I was just concentrating on not crashing the limo with POTUS inside. We left the security and lights of the White House and headed off into the inky-black night.

Only a car length behind the lead car, I stared at its taillights through what appeared to be a fishbowl with windshield wipers. This took every ounce of concentration I possessed. With no intersection control, we moved with the flow of traffic. It was tense. Along the way, we saw several accidents. The flashing lights of emergency vehicles refracted off raindrop prisms on the fishbowl making things even more distorted.

After about thirty rather exciting minutes, we arrived at Andrews. When the blue-and-white DC-9 landed—with "United States of America" painted on the fuselage—I pulled the limo near the foot of the steps. When the First Lady was about halfway down, President Clinton and Chelsea exited the limo. POTUS stood there holding flowers with a happy look. He appeared much like any other husband hoping to pleasantly surprise his wife on Valentine's Day. The First Lady was very surprised indeed.

Mrs. Clinton and the president entered the limo with Chelsea between them. The door closed and we departed for the White House. I tuned out the conversation behind me and concentrated on my sole purpose in life, delivering them all safely back to the White House.

The last major hurdle was guiding the limo around the barriers in reverse order. I wanted to get the massive vehicle onto the grounds of the White House without launching the president, the First Lady, and Chelsea into the front seat. We arrived at the South Portico where I brought the beast to a gentle stop. The detail leader whispered, "Thanks, Dan." I heard the president say, "Thank you."

"My pleasure," I responded as I breathed a silent but heavy sigh of relief. I had just delivered the leader of the free world and his family safely home.

REMAIN FLEXIBLE

The need for a Secret Service agent to remain flexible in all situations became apparent to me one dark morning in 1993 when I appeared at the White House for the day shift. I had been working many shifts with no regular day off, and was looking forward to some down time in the next day or so. It was not to be.

Upon entering the White House, I was met by my shift leader, who informed me President Clinton's mother had passed away. I was to return home and pack for a trip of undetermined duration to the president's boyhood home of Arkansas. We would be leaving on Air Force One within the next three hours, so I had to really move it.

I now had to put my personal life on hold for the next few days, the norm on PPD. I also had to deal with the stress of driving back home in rush hour traffic, packing, and returning to the White House to join my shift for the trip to Andrews Air Force Base. If I failed to make it on time, AF-1 would not wait.

The agents at the White House were to be relieved by my shift. They also had to exhibit flexibility because they had to remain on post until my shift returned ready to travel . . . this, after they had already worked a midnight shift.

Fortunately, like most agents, I always kept a bag at home with the basics for an out-of-town trip. As a result, I added a few essentials and was able to barely make it back to the White House on time.

Even with the best plans, schedules, and procedures, an agent had to remain flexible to correctly respond to situations and people. Agents always had to battle being lulled by the routine in order to stay sharp for any eventuality.

★ 8 ★

Life in the Secret Service

To the casual observer the job of a PPD agent appears glamorous and exciting. Thoughts of James Bond, martial arts, license to kill, fast cars, and martinis come to mind. The reality is quite different.

Legions of people have asked me to describe exactly what it is like to be one of the Secret Service's elite who protected three presidents. In terms of the actual physical experience, try this. First forgo sleep for twenty-four hours, skip lunch and dinner. Then, stand outside your house at 3:00 a.m. for several hours, take a cab to the airport, and board a plane for a four-hour flight to a large city.

Repeat this schedule for several days in a row. To

make the simulation complete, fail to attend a child's birthday or graduation, and miss the holidays or your wedding anniversary. With this regimen you might begin to simulate a Secret Service agent's experience.

A PPD agent's life revolves around an eight-week schedule. Like a factory worker, the routine is essentially shift work. Each agent is assigned to the presidential working shift for a two-week period on day shift. This is followed by two weeks on midnight shift, and then two weeks on the evening shift. At the end of this six-week cycle the agent goes into a two-week training phase. Then the cycle begins all over again. Changing shifts every two weeks, combined with constant travel to different time zones, is very hard on the body.

In addition to the agents who are assigned directly to the president, there are various other sections within PPD. These sections include the First Lady's detail, the First Family's detail(s), and transportation. After an agent has been on the working shift with the president for a period of time, he will be moved to another section for usually a year. After that, he can be moved back to the working shift. This at least gives an agent a break in routine and allows for a more normal existence.

Still, there are trips to every corner of the world,

announced and unannounced, which never seem to end. This on-the-go lifestyle is all part of protecting the president of the United States. I have never heard former PPD agents say they wished they had done any protection assignment other than PPD. Those of us who have survived the experience will all say it was worth it.

A TYPICAL DAY IN THE LIFE OF A PPD AGENT

Most people know that the Secret Service Presidential Protection Division (PPD) has the mission of safeguarding the president around the clock. But what does an agent actually do on a day-to-day basis? That depends entirely on the president's scheduled events for a given day. There is NO typical day.

PPD work is shift work meaning eight hours per day or sometimes more. The extra hours could be directly protecting POTUS, or serving in a support role. It is seldom glamorous work, yet very satisfying An agent is left with a tremendous sense of accomplishment at the end of a shift, even if nothing noteworthy occurred that day other than being in the White House. We on the PPD working shift were always keenly aware that without us, the president and his family would not survive for very long.

Simply *being* a part of PPD always made me proud. No matter how tired I was and regardless of anything else that was occurring in my life at the time, I became reenergized each time I approached the White House. Merely being in the same place where so much American history had happened always filled me with a sense of purpose. Nothing else in my life up to that point had done so much. Some days were very exciting . . . many others quite mundane.

When an agent reports to the White House for their shift, they usually report twenty minutes prior to going on post. This time is initially spent "gearing up," meaning donning one's pistol, radio, handcuffs, and other protective equipment. The shift briefing conducted by the senior member of the working shift follows this ritual. The agent in charge goes over the schedule for POTUS, assigns each agent their initial post. The agent in charge then briefs on actions of the shift should various emergencies occur.

If POTUS is not leaving the White House during an agent's shift, the agents engage in what is known as "ring around the Oval." Simply stated, it is the continuous standing in one place or another in close proximity to POTUS for the entire shift. Generally, an agent stands post for about eighty minutes and then gets a twenty- or sometimes forty-minute break. On such days, all agents look forward to lunchtime when they can eat a sandwich prepared by the White House mess. As I recall, the toasted chicken salad sandwich was exquisite.

Should POTUS leave the White House in a car, his agents go with him in the motorcade. Upon arriving at the site, each agent moves from the follow-up car to a post at the site designated by the site agent. Most agents welcome a trip or two during the day. Such outings break the monotony of standing post at the White House.

The least glamorous of all shifts, but perhaps one of the most important, is the midnight shift. Here, the most challenging thing for an agent is staying awake all night and most importantly, remaining alert. During these shifts the coffee flows like champagne on New Year's Eve. Agents seem to have their own system of staying focused.

I can say with certainty that during my many years with three presidents, I never saw or heard of an agent sleeping on post during a midnight shift. An agent's self-discipline takes over, even if every other instinct tells him to sleep. Each agent knows they can sleep when they get home. When protecting POTUS during these times, the president and the First Family are the only people allowed to sleep.

Perhaps the most interesting thing to occur on any shift (from an agent's point of view) is when POTUS leaves the Oval Office in the West Wing and returns to the main mansion. There is a Secret Service post very near the Oval Office. Whenever POTUS leaves the Oval for his walk back to the mansion, the agent standing at this post accompanies POTUS to the residence and into the elevator. Some of my most vivid memories of being on PPD are escorting POTUS on these movements. During these times, it was not unusual for POTUS to initiate conversation. The topics were general, or could be more personal. I do not believe any agent was unaware they were having a conversation with the leader of the free world. This was a very special privilege.

TRAINING, ALWAYS TRAINING

Even after reporting to one of the two major protective details, the Presidential Protection Division (PPD) and the Vice Presidential Protection Division (VPPD), each agent undergoes training every eight weeks. Known as Protective Detail Training (PDT), the two-week stint keeps agents sharp in all related skills while remaining in top physical condition. During this time, agents requalify with their service pistol, submachine gun, and shotgun. They retake the physical fitness test consisting of push-ups, pull-ups, abdominal crunches, and a timed 1.5-mile run. A refresher in medical emergencies is also given to every agent.

The final day of PDT is spent in Attack on a Principal (AOP) exercise. Agents must respond to mock attacks that simulate assaults on their protectee. These attacks could include responding to a lone gunman on a rope line, dealing with a long-distance shooter, or handling a medical emergency. One drill is a water emergency, such as exiting a crashed helicopter. In this scenario, several agents are seated blindfolded in a device that simulates a helicopter fuselage submerged in water. The fuselage is then rolled and inverted. Agents must swim out of the simulated helicopter with no visual reference on one breath of air while fighting panic.

The problems are a bit different every time, so no one can really guess what will come next. All agents, including supervisors, participate. It is without doubt the finest protective training in the world. It is also the major reason the Secret Service has been so successful in protecting the nation's leaders over the decades.

A UNIQUE RELATIONSHIP

The relationship between the president and Secret Service agents is complicated. Presidents exist in a world where many who surround them are seeking personal gain. Loyalties can be bought with promises of power. Given a president's constant association with these kinds of individuals, I believe they find it refreshing that their agents have a pure commitment to something greater than themselves. Perhaps another thing some presidents realize is although they may be president, they most likely could not qualify to be a Secret Service agent.

One of the most misunderstood relationships in the world is that of an American president and the Secret Service agents who surround him. Each respects the other. The relationship is not one of friendship, but can be misinterpreted by all but the most professional of agents.

This is a complex relationship so puzzling that even experienced agents who have seen more than one president come and go find it difficult to understand. It can also be extremely awkward for both new president and new PPD agent alike. Rookie PPD agents—when spoken to by POTUS for the first time—can be a bit starstruck. Sometimes in that situation, an agent tends to talk a bit too much. A new agent must avoid this at all costs.

In no case does POTUS's reaching out to speak to an agent mean a wish to be friends. Any agent who mistakenly believes that such a gesture is one of friendship will not last long on the detail.

This unique relationship of protector and pro-tected is based on the idea that the president is in the business of being president while the Secret Service is in the business of protecting the president. Agents are physically close to POTUS every day. An agent hears and sees almost everything the president sees and hears. Unlike the presidential staff that interacts with POTUS, Secret Service agents stand silently and only offer input on security-related matters.

If asked by POTUS about a situation, especially political, the agent should be brief and friendly, yet noncommittal. An agent is not to begin a conversa-tion with the president except to be polite. Should the president wish to talk to an agent, it is important for the agent to converse out of respect for the office of the presidency. The agent is not to become too chatty. Many times POTUS is merely being friendly and does not want to have a long conversation.

On one occasion, a First Lady of the United States (FLOTUS) asked an agent an unimportant question while escorting a group of women through the Rose Garden. The agent went far beyond the required polite response, to the point of practically becoming a part of the tour group. One week later the agent was reassigned to a post other than PPD. The best policy for a PPD agent is to speak as little as possible to POTUS or FLOTUS while remaining approachable.

Familiarity between POTUS and FLOTUS with their agents can be a detriment to security and is to be avoided. While presidents and First Ladies are aware of an agent's job, each has staff that works for them. Agents can sometimes be placed in a difficult position requiring the agent to be tactful and diplomatic.

For example, a First Lady asked her agent in charge to have an agent retrieve her makeup bag from the limo. This is a staff function that could distract the agent from the primary purpose—protection. However, the staffer was not as close as the agent. The agent did not say, "Sorry, that is not a Secret Service function." An answer like that would cause friction. In this case, the agent simply nodded, then sent a radio call to his detail to locate the First Lady's staff and pass along the request.

The Secret Service does not work for the president. The PPD serves a purpose. If an agent becomes too close to a president, that closeness could cloud an agent's professional judgment in a crisis. Secret Service agents work for the director of the Secret Service and the Secretary of the Department of Homeland Security.

An agent is assigned to PPD, not to the person who is president. When a president leaves office, the agents who have protected him do not then move on to his post-presidential detail. The agent remains on PPD to protect the new president. I saw this firsthand in 1992 as a PPD agent in the George H. W. Bush administration. When President Bush lost the general election to President Clinton, Bush picked up an entirely new group of agents. His old protectors, including me, watched over President Clinton.

Some PPD agents protect people other than the president. These small details within the presidential detail have one thing in common—each protectee has a direct line to the president.

Agents who watch over the president's children have a very hard task at times. Historically, children of POTUS have had a wide range of ages and temperaments, from young children such as Caroline and John Kennedy Jr. and Amy Carter to adults such as the Reagan, Ford, Johnson, Nixon, and Bush children. In between are teenage and college-age children such as Jenna and Barbara Bush or Sasha and

Malia Obama. Each famous child of a president has his or her own distinct personality.

Often, these children may not want to be controlled by the Secret Service in any way. While POTUS may not always enjoy the restrictions placed upon his activities, he understands the need for it. Children of POTUS sometimes do not. As such, some resent the imposing, always present Secret Service in their lives. This agent presence makes a normal life all but impossible.

The threat against these children of POTUS is not so much assassination as kidnapping. Imagine the impossible situation a president would be in should his child be abducted and held for demands that could never be met. Because of this, agents assigned to the seemingly unimportant children's detail must be as vigilant as those assigned to the president himself.

This assignment is made more difficult when a child complains to his or her father—the president—that the Secret Service is ruining his personal life. The president may make it even harder by asking the Secret Service to give his child more space. Too much space can be the same as too little protection. The agents bear the responsibility if something happens to his charge.

A PPD must be a mix of bodyguard and diplomat. The agent must be prepared to handle any crisis, be it a gunshot or complaining adolescent.

AN AGENT'S PERSONAL LIFE

While a member of PPD, an agent's life completely ceases to be his or her own. The agent's life becomes the sole property of the Secret Service and the office of the presidency. The term "family-friendly" will never apply to those entrusted with the life of the president.

Single agents fare better than those with a spouse. While an agent may be married with children, there really is no family outside the Secret Service family. An agent may have a house, but his true home is the White House.

A PPD agent is free to plan family outings, vacations, and dinners. However, he should not be disappointed or even surprised when plans have to be canceled. Sometimes this happens at the last possible moment. In some cases, plans have been scrapped as an agent and family were on the way to the airport to enjoy a vacation.

For the agent, it is all part of the job. For spouses and children, these last-minute calls are impossible to understand. "Why can't they find someone else?"

asks a spouse who is soothing a tearful child who doesn't understand why the beach trip or ball game outing is canceled.

In December 1992, President George H. W. Bush, who had just lost the election, was to travel to Russia and France on January 2, 1993. The trip had been planned for a long time. The advance teams had already deployed. Those not involved were looking forward to a few days with family for Christmas. At the last moment, President Bush unexpectedly decided to start his trip with stops in Saudi Arabia and Somalia on December 31st.

To cover the advances for these new stops (and to man the required CAT teams and working shifts) scores of PPD agents with approved Christmas leave were recalled. This trip required all agents on the detail. Many agents who had already arrived at holiday destinations were contacted and told to pack for a foreign trip.

As the CAT operations agent, I had to write a new schedule in a matter of hours. I had spent five days writing the one that was now the "old" schedule! I had to call several agents back to Washington from their holidays. This was a difficult assignment.

All the agents whose Christmas leave was canceled were frustrated with the last-minute change. I patiently listened to their anger and resentment before giving each agent his travel itinerary. The deafening echoes of exploding spouses, crushed grandparents, and upset children could be heard all the way to the White House.

What makes this part of the work bearable is that everyone on PPD makes the same sacrifice. Because of common hardships, unbreakable bonds form between these remarkable people that last a lifetime. Sadly, in some cases, the friendships last longer than the marriages of some agents.

THE AGENT WHO LOVED ME . . . EVENTUALLY

To be a married Secret Service agent seemed like a lot of work and trouble. The realities of the job made being a good husband and father seemingly impossible. I knew I loved the Secret Service, but I merely enjoyed the company of attractive women. I was a confirmed bachelor. Nothing could change that. However, I came face to face with the reality of "never say never."

In November 1988, I was assigned to advance preparations for the visit of Mikhail Gorbachev, General Secretary of the Communist Party of the Soviet Union. Part of my assignment was to meet an agent from the San Francisco office who would assist the advance team in interpreting Russian.

I went to the Vista Hotel to pick up this agent who turned out to be a very attractive female. As she got into my car, she said, "Hi, my name is Donnelle."

"Hi, I—I . . . am Dan," I stammered.

Up close she was even more beautiful than I had first thought. Over the next several days, her beauty, along with the scent of her perfume, nearly drove me to distraction. I had to concentrate on the business of moving Russians safely around New York. It took all my professional discipline to complete this assignment.

During those few short days Donnelle and I worked closely together. While I tried my best to impress her with whatever charm I could muster, she seemed uninterested. Even so, we became friends. When it came time for her to return to San Francisco, I sadly thought I had seen the last of her.

Over the next year, Donnelle and I stayed in touch but never saw each other. When I transferred to CAT, I made several trips to San Francisco. Each time I was with Donnelle, I liked her more and more. In the spring of 1990, Donnelle came to Washington once again to translate for a visit of Mikhail Gorbachev, by then the president of the Soviet Union.

During that assignment, I took up as much of Donnelle's after-hours time as possible. One of the benefits of socializing with other agents is that we all have the same security clearances and can talk "shop." Donnelle and I talked for hours on end, never seeming to run out of things to say.

One evening at supper, I asked, "How was your day interpreting for the Russians?"

"The Russians are fun to work with," she said with a smile. "I had been interpreting when one of the Russian Counter Assault Team members came up to me. He spoke to me in English instead of Russian. He said, 'All day we have been called CAT. We do not know why we are called CAT. Can you please tell us why we are called CAT? Is this bad?'"

She then told me that she wrote on a piece of paper in Russian that CAT simply stood for Counter Assault Team. The Russian seemed pleased. "Thank you," he said. "We now know why we are called CAT." She said that he showed the paper to his team. Chests expanded as each Russian CAT member smiled and nodded. They obviously were proud of the new title.

As she told this amusing story, I realized that one of the most important things in a relationship, one I had been missing, was having things in common with the other person. One evening after dinner, I unexpectedly blurted out, "Hypothetically, if I were to ask you to marry me, what would you say?"

"Hypothetically, perhaps," she answered. She then told me she would be in Dallas the following month to protect George W. Bush, son of President George H. W. Bush.

"I didn't know we were protecting him," I said. "Doesn't he own the Texas Rangers baseball team?"

"Right," she offered. "Stop changing the subject. If you are serious, non-hypothetically, you could come to Dallas in June and ask me."

I traveled to Dallas that June and proposed to this Italian American beauty. To my surprise, she accepted. To my astonishment, I was now engaged to be married and very happy about it all.

Two Secret Service agents marrying one another is not an easy proposition. She was, after all, stationed on the West Coast, and I in Washington, DC. Donnelle accepting my proposal was only half the battle. Now, the Secret Service was going to have to cooperate. At that time, the Service policy stated that spouses could not serve in the same office or division. This made marriage between agents difficult.

It was hard, but we worked out all the details. The Secret Service operations in Washington were so large it was possible for both of us to work there without being in the same office. As our wedding date neared, it appeared that one or both of us might not make it to the ceremony for several reasons. Three days before we were to be married, Donnelle was in Colombia, South America, and I was in Haiti.

Somehow, it all came together, although I have no idea how. On November 10, 1990, we were married in my hometown, Gainesville, Georgia. November 10th is the Marine Corps birthday. Being married on that particular day ensured I would never forget our anniversary. Semper Fi.

After our honeymoon in Hilton Head, South Carolina, we moved into my small condo in Maryland. Since one of us was usually gone most of the time, our marriage seemed like a never-ending honeymoon or the greatest date in the world. It is a date that has lasted for over two decades and produced the finest son anyone could wish for.

THE WHITE HOUSE CHRISTMAS PARTY

The one night of the year a PPD agent and spouse look forward to most is the annual White House Christmas party. Being a POTUS party guest is a perk of being a member of PPD. For one night, an agent is treated as a presidential guest rather than a presidential protector.

Other than high rollers from headquarters, the only Secret Service agents invited to these galas are PPD agents. This party is the president's way of thanking the men and women who would sacrifice anything to protect him and his family from harm. These holiday parties were great for morale and almost made up for all the bad coffee consumed trying to stay awake during midnight shifts.

Each agent is allowed to bring one guest. Few date invitations can equal being invited to accompany a Secret Service agent to the White House. Cocktails, dancing, and a photo op with the president and First Lady are special indeed.

Bringing a parent to this special event will usually produce forgiveness for any misdeeds of youth. As a side note, the complete absolution of *my* youthful transgressions came when I arranged a meeting between my parents and President George Herbert Walker Bush. It happened in 1992 as President Bush passed through my hometown of Gainesville. Sadly, the White House photographer's equipment malfunctioned, and no record exists of the meeting. It was a moment my parents cherished for the rest of their lives.

At the White House Christmas party, all guests enter through the East Entrance. Everyone moves through the East Wing and into the lower level of the main mansion. An impeccably dressed, commissioned officer of one of the armed forces directs guests up a well-worn set of marble stairs. Millions have ascended this staircase since it was installed in 1953.

On one occasion, a Navy SEAL lieutenant, due to leave the navy because of numerous disabilities, manned this post. At the age of twenty-six, this young man had sustained so many broken bones and torn ligaments as a SEAL he was no longer medically qualified. Being around such men is always humbling. I felt he should have been the president's guest instead of me.

At the top of the staircase, guests proceed to the state floor of the mansion for the festivities. Christmas decorations and several large, live Christmas trees fill the area. Guests move about through the East Room, Green Room, Blue Room, Red Room, and State Dining Room. An enormous, white-cloth-covered table filled with hors d'oeuvres runs the length of the State Dining Room.

A military orchestra in the East Room provides a variety of music. Some guests simply listen, while others dance. This is where Donnelle's and my Arthur Murray training always paid off.

The president and First Lady descend the main stairs where they mingle with their guests. From there POTUS and FLOTUS move to the photo op area where they graciously stand for an hour or more. Each guest is announced prior to their photo with the president and First Lady.

The photo op is generally the grand finale of the evening. After the last guest is posed, things start to wind down. Being lucky enough to attend even one of these events provides a very special lifetime memory. Donnelle and I were privileged to have attended six such evenings in our careers.

★ **9** ★

I Am a Secret Service Agent

After I had been protecting presidents full-time for over five years, my tour in the transportation section was coming to an end. Soon, I would return to the working shift. Instead, I asked for a transfer from PPD to the Atlanta field office. I had done everything I came to Washington to do. Now it was time to turn the page.

My transfer came through, not to Atlanta, but to the Washington field office. When I found this out, I asked to stay on PPD. That did not work out, either. Instead, I was offered an assignment as an instructor in the training division.

During the eleven years I had been an agent, I

realized that while protecting the president was still the most important thing the Secret Service did, it was not the *only* important thing. Presidential protection is not something a person can do indefinitely. Even the strongest people have their limits. The Secret Service had many other vital jobs. Training each new group of young people as agents was critically important.

I had enjoyed my years on CAT and PPD more than I can describe. I was now headed to a worthwhile assignment where I could pass on some of the knowledge I had gained.

I checked out of PPD on a Friday. The following Monday my wife replaced me. At the same moment she was putting her gear into my old cubby inside White House Command Post W-16, I was checking into the Special Agent Training Education Division at 1310 L Street. Over the next nine years, I helped train over two thousand new Secret Service agents.

The important thing as an instructor was to teach from a position of having done, in real time, what you were teaching. New students gave you their attention and respect as long as you had actually performed the subject matter in a genuine setting. Many of the students had vast law enforcement and military experience.

Students picked up on the fact when an instructor did not have actual experience and was only reading from notes or slides. I could always pull out a story about driving President Clinton, riding in the follow-up, working a rope line, or traveling on an advance. Most of the men wanted to know about CAT and how to get there.

I told each class they needed to listen to me for two reasons: 1) I only taught what they actually needed to know; and 2) if they didn't pay attention, they would fail and be sent home.

I taught physical fitness and protection to all Special Agent Training Classes (SATC). As always, I did my best to prepare these young men and women to survive in a world that is not politically correct. In that world, there are those who kill because a person carries a badge. None of those predators care if the carrier of the badge is a man or a woman. I was determined that no student under my instruction and leadership would ever meet such a fate because I had not done enough to prepare them.

AMERICA AT WAR

On Tuesday, September 11, 2001, I was teaching a practical exercise when an instructor told me an airliner had flown into the World Trade Center. I had a bad feeling it was not an accident. While assigned to New York, I had many times rented a plane and flown up the Hudson River corridor past the World Trade Center. There was no way even a poor pilot could accidentally fly into either tower in the midst of that day's perfect weather.

As I continued with my class, another instructor brought news that a second plane had flown into the other tower of the World Trade Center. I knew we were at war. I guessed Osama bin Laden and al-Qaeda were behind it.

America was catching hell on 9/11, and I knew the training division was about to catch hell as well. The automatic response of the US government in times of violent crisis is to hire more people. The Secret Service began hiring agents in record numbers to fill the newly authorized slots. This meant we would be training classes of recruits six days per week for the near future.

PROMOTION AND RETURN TO PPD

One uneventful day in 2002, as I was teaching, my boss walked into the classroom. He told me I had been promoted to assistant to the special agent in charge in the training division. He walked out and left me with my class. I was happy to finally be promoted, but I had not been expecting this. I was a bit in shock for the rest of the class as well as the rest of the day.

The director of the Secret Service called to congratulate me. I appreciated his taking the time to call, and I thanked him for his personal involvement. Afterward, I sat at my desk and, in spite of the No Smoking signs, opened a window and lit a cigar.

Even though I could retire in only one more year, I decided I wanted to get back to PPD for one last operational assignment. I had spent far too long as an instructor. Many thought I had been away from the operational side of the house so long that teaching was all I could do. Maybe they were right, but I wanted the chance to find out.

In August of the next year, I requested a transfer to PPD. I was selected for reassignment as one of two supervisors in charge of CAT. After a nine-year absence, I was returning to protection. I reported back to PPD and CAT. For almost a decade, I had taught others how to protect presidents and how to get and stay in shape. Now I was back to helping accomplish the most important mission of the Secret Service—protecting the president of the United States.

A few months after coming back to PPD, I had to make a major decision. Since I was eligible for retirement, I began to look for a post–Secret Service assignment within the federal government. It was not unusual for Secret Service agents to retire and work for the newly formed Transportation Security Administration or the Treasury Department. I was not really interested in those jobs.

Since 9/11, I had wanted to contribute in an active way to the war on terror. My thoughts turned to America's main intelligence service, the Central Intelligence Agency (CIA). The CIA manned the front lines in the war on terror. This is where I felt I could best serve.

I applied to the CIA fearing that I might be a little too old. I was to discover that the CIA had no age limits for practically any job. Their only concern was attracting the best people for a myriad of jobs. As long as a person was physically qualified for the position, all was good to go.

9/11 had occurred two years earlier, and the CIA was in full hiring mode. Three weeks after applying, I had a message from a CIA recruiting officer. The following week I was sitting in a CIA building taking a written exam. Over the next several months I underwent a battery of testing, interviews, psychological exams, and a very brutal full-scope polygraph exam.

One afternoon as I was sitting in my office, the phone rang. The CIA recruiting officer called to inform me I had been accepted for the position. It was déjà vu all over again. I sat at my desk with much the same feeling of anticipation I'd had two decades earlier when the SAIC of Atlanta had called to inform me I had been accepted into the Secret Service.

Now, with twenty-one years as a Secret Service agent and a career poised for advancement, I had a very big decision to make. Stay with the Secret Service and enjoy the soft life of management? Or retire and move to the CIA, where I would be back in the game, albeit as the world's oldest rookie.

A large part of the decision involved what my wife thought about the venture. My leaving the Secret Service for the CIA was not only a career risk, but a real one as well. The first American killed in Afghanistan was a CIA officer and former Marine Corps captain, Johnny Spann. As a husband and father, I was not certain I had the right to take that kind of risk. Donnelle's attitude was the same as it had always been. If becoming a part of the CIA was what I wanted, she would support it.

In my den late that evening, wearing a Marine Corps sweatshirt and PT shorts, the last fire of the season burned. I sat with my thoughts and a twelve-year-old scotch. Staring at the flames, I played back my entire career—from when I first dreamed of becoming a Secret Service agent to the present.

I weighed the fact that a Secret Service agent was all I had been for the past twenty-one years. Once I pulled the pin to retire, there was no putting it back. I thought about these and many other things until very late, and then went to bed. Sleep did not come easily. When morning arrived, the feeling from the night before was still firmly in place. As illogical as it seemed, I decided to retire from the Secret Service and join the CIA.

LAST NIGHT AT THE WHITE HOUSE

My final two weeks in the Secret Service I served as an acting shift leader on the midnight shift at the White House and on weekends at Camp David, the presidential retreat. It was the perfect way to close my Secret Service career.

I had first entered the White House as a CAT agent fifteen years earlier. Now I was responsible for the safety of the president and First Lady, who slept upstairs in the second-floor residence. I was responsible for the immediate action of getting the president and First Lady to safety between the hours of 10:00 p.m. and 6:00 a.m.—no matter the emergency.

On my last night as an agent, in the quiet of the midnight routine, I walked about the silent dimness of the mansion. I thought of all the years I had worked there. In many ways, the White House felt like home. During some periods, I spent more time there than at my actual home.

I remembered the three presidents I had protected. I reflected on my years in CAT, the working shift, running and driving with President Clinton, and the Christmas parties Donnelle and I had attended. Also, I thought of all the friends I made there, some no longer living. When morning came, it was difficult to walk out for the last time.

In a small ceremony at the Old Executive Office Building, I officially retired from the Secret Service. My wife and son were with me. It was May 16, 2004, twenty-one years to the day after I took the oath of office in Charlotte, North Carolina. Many friends from PPD attended. Some young agents from CAT whom I had supervised and trained came as well.

My good friend John Mrha presented each award and plaque due an agent at retirement. The main retirement plaque, which is the Secret Service equivalent of a gold watch, reads in part:

> Your twenty-one years of dedication and contributions to the missions and goals of the United States Secret Service are hereby gratefully acknowledged and affirm you to be worthy of trust and confidence.

My family and I left the proceedings and walked to our car outside the White House. The Secret Service was behind me. New adventures and challenges awaited me at the CIA. It was an exciting time.

TAKING THE OATH AT THE CIA

Only six weeks later, I stood in CIA Headquarters at Langley with a group of new officers. A deputy director told us to raise our right hand, and we repeated back to him the oath of office. It was the same oath I had taken to become a Marine Corps officer and to become a Secret Service agent.

In my first twenty months at the CIA, I was assigned to the Directorate of Operations. My first job there was in the Counterintelligence Center (CIC) where I helped ferret out those whose motives for being in the CIA were questionable. Next, I worked in the Counterterrorism Center (CTC) focused on the current war.

The art of espionage is unique. Although I would never become a master spy, I did learn the basics of espionage, tradecraft, and CIA weaponry. I also learned how to incapacitate an enemy in any number of ways.

In the Secret Service (a law enforcement agency), agents trained in defensive tactics. They learned the use of minimum force to subdue an opponent. At the CIA, an intelligence service, we trained in offensive tactics. This meant learning to kill quickly and efficiently using any object at our disposal. There were no rules of engagement or concerns over legal issues for killing an enemy in a foreign land. I moved from an escalation model to a new doctrine of kill rather than subdue.

OFF TO WAR

After learning some of the basics, I became a deputy branch chief in the Counterterrorism Center (CTC). This group was active in the war against terrorism. I knew it was only a matter of time before I would be

"on the tip of the spear." This is what I had volunteered for.

One quiet morning, Donnelle left our house for
her job at Secret Service headquarters. I took our son
to daycare and came home. I watched as my neighbors went about their lives doing whatever people do
when they are not in the Secret Service or the CIA.
I sat in the same chair in which I had made the decision to retire from the Secret Service and join the
CIA. The grandfather clock ticked in the hall. I
penned a letter to my wife and son. I was so engrossed
in my thoughts, I failed to notice the taxi in our
driveway. The taxi's horn snapped me back into the
moment. I picked up my bag and headed out the front
door for the CIA's war in Afghanistan.

THE TIP OF THE SPEAR

Uncomfortably cold on a dreary morning in late
winter, I stood drinking the world's worst coffee.
Two other members of the CIA's National Clandes-
tine Service joined me at a CIA base camp. We were
somewhere in the infinite expanse of Afghanistan.

As a deputy branch chief, I was in Afghanistan to
aid my branch in its mission and assess its needs. I
wanted to get dirty and function as a working mem-

ber of the group. Not long in country, I suffered from the mother of all jet lags (we were 9.5 hours earlier than Washington, DC, time). I shook the cobwebs out of my head and prepared for what was not exactly a normal day at the office.

Temperatures were beginning to rise as spring approached in this primitive land. However, snow still covered the rugged peaks that divided Afghanistan from Pakistan. The stark mountain beauty is not found in other parts of the world. I marveled at its majesty as I prepared for the day's work. The serenity of the jagged snow-covered peaks was deceptive.

These ancient mountains were home to the Taliban and al-Qaeda. Countless caves seemingly custom-made for terrorists existed throughout this terrain. The terrorists could ambush with small arms fire, rocket attack, and Improvised Explosive Devices (IEDs). Then they disappeared back into the holes from which they came.

For ten years America and the CIA had helped these people in their war against the Soviet Union. Now the United States and its CIA was the enemy of these very same people. That was then. This is now. It was the classic example of how certain events can cause old friends to become enemies. Twenty-five years earlier in a struggle against the Soviets, these people would have welcomed us. Now they might cut off our heads with rusty blades given half a chance.

This was not the gentleman's CIA of cocktail parties, martinis, and tuxedos. In *that* CIA, if the enemy apprehended an officer, he would simply be sent back to the United States. But Afghanistan was the workingman's CIA. Dirt, cold, heat, bad food, and never-ending danger were an officer's constant companions. If captured, we would be tortured, used for propaganda, and slaughtered like goats.

I dumped the last of my cold coffee on the frozen Afghan ground and slipped into body armor. Next, I shrugged on the load-bearing vest with spare ammunition magazines, knife, radio, and a Glock pistol. Joints and ligaments, stiff from decades of abuse in physical fitness training, protested, as I pulled on my equipment in the freezing dawn.

I made sure I had my all-important Snickers bar in one pouch. I placed my Colt M4 carbine—loaded with a thirty-round magazine, stock collapsed and muzzle down—between the driver's seat and the right front seat of the lightly armored SUV. I climbed into the driver's seat and started the engine. This vehicle would carry our group on a potentially deadly assignment. With a silent prayer, off we went into the breach.

We left the relative safety of our covert base. I avoided many mortar impact craters on the road. Some of these craters dated back to the Soviet occupation. I constantly scanned the terrain for possible ambush sites. I also followed the prescribed procedures to detect anyone who might have been following us. This was important, since the only thing keeping us alive on a daily basis was the secrecy of our location.

I remembered our group chief's final pre-deployment mission briefing back in the safety of CIA Headquarters. Before we left for the most dangerous country in the world, he reminded us our primary mission was to gather intelligence that would prevent another 9/11. We were not to seek out the enemy for a fight. We also were reminded that our secondary mission was to capture or kill any top-level members of al-Qaeda. During the time of its existence, our group was very successful in both the primary and secondary missions.

Back in DC that day, as the boss walked out of the briefing, he said over his shoulder, "One final thing. Never get caught by this enemy." Having seen video and still photos of some who had been captured, I thought it was excellent advice.

Al-Qaeda had begun using the age-old tactic of placing fake checkpoints along routes traveled by Americans. Once a vehicle had stopped, it was either attacked by automatic weapons or the occupants were captured and later executed. While actual Afghan security forces manned checkpoints, there was no way to tell if certain checkpoints were traps. So we never stopped at any checkpoint unless it was clearly manned by Americans or UN forces.

A few hours later, our mission of the day complete, we began the trip back to base with darkness falling. It was never a good idea to be driving the back roads of Afghanistan, even in the daylight. We hurried along as the sun set. We were always careful to make sure we were not being followed. As we rounded a curve we saw a checkpoint less than one hundred yards away. Americans definitely did not man it.

I began to accelerate the SUV. I quickly assessed whether it would be best to drive straight through the threat or risk hitting a mine by going off the road. At a glance, I realized that both sides of the checkpoint dropped off into a steep drainage ditches. This made the decision for me. We would go through.

As I continued to speed toward the flimsy barricade, an Afghan in battle dress uniform with a Kalashnikov rifle slung across his chest squared off at the checkpoint. He raised one hand like a traffic cop. I had already made my decision as to my course of action. The soldier now had to make his. He had to decide whether to live or die on this late afternoon in Afghanistan.

Back at base that evening, I thought about the events of the day, our mission for the next day, and my current situation. Meanwhile, back in Washington at the CAT office, a close friend I had recommended as my replacement was sitting in my comfortable chair signing paperwork and watching the war on Fox News. I remembered the old saying: *Be careful what you wish for, you just might get it.*

★ **10** ★

The Secret Service Today

Young people often ask, "How do I become a Secret Service agent?" My own story illustrates one of the many ways to become an agent. Many of my fellow agents began their career in the military. Others started in law enforcement at the local and state level. Still others worked in emergency response. Men and women from various backgrounds decide to make a career with the Secret Service. There really is no "one size fits all." The Secret Service strives for a qualified highly diverse agent pool.

There are many intangible qualities not officially listed, such as personal appearance and good speech diction. The actual qualifications can be found on

the Secret Service Web site (www.SecretService.
gov). The Web site did not exist during my application process as there was no Internet. Still, the basic
qualifications remain largely unchanged since my entry into the Secret Service. One major difference lies
in the visual acuity requirement. My group was required to possess 20/40 acuity in each eye correctable
to 20/20. Today the requirement has been relaxed to
20/60 and Lasik surgery correction is permitted.

According to the Web site "candidates must be US
citizens and must submit to urinalysis screening for
illegal drug use." Also, all Secret Service positions require a Top Secret security clearance. Physical fitness,
good vision, and excellent health are also required. A
young person should avoid the criminal element and
always respect and abide by the law. Remember—
"you are known by the company you keep." An applicant must pass the polygraph (lie detector) regarding
criminal activity in order to be accepted. Merely not
getting caught committing serious crimes and having
no record, is not good enough. A Secret Service agent
is a law enforcement officer. One cannot enforce the
law if one has been a habitual violator of the law.

A future agent should do their best in school and
produce the highest Grade Point Average (GPA) possible in college. In some cases, when all things are

equal, a person with a 3.3 GPA will be hired over the applicant with the 3.2 GPA. In today's world, GPA is very important.

Not all agents protect the president and the First Family. Members of the Uniformed Division protect the buildings and sites secured for Secret Service protectees. For instance, the Uniformed Division guards the White House and other venues.

The Administrative, Professional, and Technical (APT) Division ensures the Secret Service's overall success. APT works behind the scenes to keep records, do research, and use science to investigate and analyze evidence. This division supports the more visible work of the special agents and special officers.

Currently, the Secret Service employs over 3,200 special agents, 1,300 Uniformed Division officers, and 2,000 other specialized administrative, professional, and technical support personnel. The Web site says that "careers with the Secret Service are challenging and demanding, yet exciting and rewarding all at the same time."

A prospective agent usually has a bachelor's degree and other experience in related fields. Also, the applicant must go through extensive interviews, a strenuous physical fitness exam, and tests that focus on necessary skills.

When a person is hired as a new special agent, he or she begins his or her career in a field office as I did in Charlotte and New York. There are sixty-eight field offices throughout the United States, as well as nineteen foreign offices. In the field office, a new agent usually investigates financial crimes, as well as government check forgery. However, an agent can also serve on *temporary* protective details.

Counterfeit suppression is one of the Service's main investigative missions. While these investigations get little media attention, they can be extremely dangerous, and one can unexpectedly be injured or even killed while conducting them.

The time in field offices is really an agent's tryout for protection details. After an agent serves approximately six years in a field office conducting investigations, he or she may move to a full-time protective assignment. An agent must prove to be trustworthy, intelligent, proficient with weapons, and hardworking. Otherwise, it is unlikely the agent will ever see the Presidential Protection Division.

The law mandates the following will receive protection:

- The president of the United States and immediate family

- The vice president and immediate family
- The president-elect and vice president-elect and immediate families
- Former presidents and their spouses for life (as well as children under age twelve)
- Major presidential candidates
- Visiting foreign heads of state in the United States on official state visits
- Anyone else the president so declares

Only the president and vice president *must* accept Secret Service protection. All others may decline protection if they choose.

MY FAVORITE PRESIDENT

I have been asked, "Of the three presidents you protected while assigned to PPD, who was your favorite?" Meaning, which one did you personally like the best?

The three presidents I directly protected—George Herbert Walker Bush, William Jefferson Clinton, and George Walker Bush—had their own personalities, likes, dislikes, and habits. Professionally speaking, all were easy to work with. Each seemed to understand and appreciate the role of the Secret Service in their lives.

Each was well aware that without the Secret Service, neither they nor their families would be safe. They understood agents were prepared to give up their own lives if necessary to save theirs. They also grasped the fact that most of us had families from whom we were away on the president's behalf.

Others have said various presidents were difficult to deal with. A few agents claimed to dislike some presidents. This was not true during my career. In reality, most agents will never become close enough to presidents or their families to either like or dislike them on a personal level.

The presidents I protected had good and bad days at the office and in their personal lives. Even on their worst days, they always treated agents with courtesy and respect. If the president or a member of his family happened to walk by without speaking or failed to thank us for our service, we did not feel insulted. We experienced no feelings at all one way or the other.

Doing whatever was necessary to ensure the president's safety was our primary job. We expected no thanks. However, the three presidents I protected (and their families) frequently offered it. We were not there to be their best friends or social equals. We were there to safeguard their lives and were thanked twice a month by the Secret Service when we received our pay.

I liked and admired each president I protected for his individual strengths. I recognized that each was a human being doing the best he could under extremely difficult circumstances. As one who has been inside the operations of three administrations, I can say that being president of the United States is the most difficult job in the world.

MISSION ACCOMPLISHED WITH NO REGRETS

When I retired in 2004, twenty years had passed since that November day when I stood alone in President Kennedy's house in Hyannis Port contemplating his cuff links. Many great things had happened in my life and career during those two decades. I had fulfilled my childhood dream of protecting not one but three presidents. I'd also had the good fortune of finding the perfect wife. I am constantly reminded, how lucky I am to have been a Secret Service agent.

I attained my career goals through a determination to succeed. This was hardwired into my DNA at birth. My parents instilled a work ethic that the Marine Corps welded into place. Any disappointments over unmet goals have been erased by a deep gratitude for those that came to pass. Even taking the road less traveled, I had no regrets.

At the age of forty-nine, I got to be part of the CIA. Alongside some of the most intelligent and courageous people anywhere in the world, I contributed in a small way to keeping America safe from terrorist attack.

I now enjoy retirement from government service and the many blessings of freedom this great country has to offer. I often think of the Secret Service agents and CIA officers I served with both at home and half a world away. Some have been lost in the fight, while many others are still poised on the tip of the spear. Godspeed, my brothers and sisters in arms.

Almost everyone has some regrets at the end of a long career in the autumn of life. Some people question career decisions or lament that more promotions did not come. Others wish perhaps they had chosen a different course altogether. I have only one wish regarding my career choice and the experiences that came as part and parcel of it. *I wish I could do it all again.*

Assassinations of United States Presidents

Abraham Lincoln	16th President	April 14, 1865 (d. 4/15/65)
James A. Garfield	20th President	July 2, 1881 (d. 9/19/81)
William McKinley	25th President	September 6, 1901 (d. 9/14/01)
John F. Kennedy	35th President	November 22, 1963

Attempted Assassinations
of United States Presidents

Andrew Jackson	7th President	January 30, 1835
Abraham Lincoln	16th President	February 23, 1861
		August 1864
William Howard Taft	27th President	October 10, 1909
Theodore Roosevelt	26th President	October 14, 1912
Herbert Hoover	31st President	November 19, 1928
Franklin D. Roosevelt	32nd President	February 15, 1933*
Harry S. Truman	33rd President	Summer 1947*
		November 1, 1950
Richard Nixon	37th President	February 22, 1974*

Attempted Assassinations of US Presidents

Gerald Ford	38th President	September 5, 1975
		September 22, 1975
Ronald Reagan	40th President	March 30, 1981
George H. W. Bush	41st President	April 13, 1993★
Bill Clinton	42nd President	January 21, 1994★
		September 12, 1994★
		October 29, 1994★
		November 1996★
George W. Bush	43rd President	May 10, 2005★
Barack Obama	44th President	November 11, 2011★
		April 15, 2013★

★Denotes plots that were foiled by the US Secret Service before an attempt was made.

★

Secret Service History Timeline

1865, July 5   The Secret Service is created to combat the widespread counterfeiting of currency after the Civil War.

1874   First United States Secret Service Commission Book issued.

1881, July 2   President James Garfield assassinated. Died on September 19th.

1894   Conducted informal protection of President Grover Cleveland

1901, September 6   President William McKinley assassinated. Died on September 14th.

1901   Congress mandates protection of the president by the Secret Service in the wake of President McKinley's assassination.

1902   Full-time protection of the president begins. Two men are stationed at the White House.

1902, September 3   Secret Service Agent William Craig is killed in a streetcar accident in Pittsfield, Massachusetts, while protecting President Theodore Roosevelt. Agent Craig is the first agent to die while protecting a president.

1908   Protection of the president-elect is added.

1917   Congress authorizes protection of the president's immediate family.

1922   White House Police Force is created.

1930   White House Police Force becomes a part of the Secret Service.

1951   Congress authorizes the protection of the vice president upon request.

1953   First formal Special Agent Training (three weeks).

1962   Vice presidential protection is mandated as well as for the vice president-elect. Protection of former presidents upon request.

1963, November 22   Assassination of President John F. Kennedy in Dallas, Texas.

1965   Congress passed legislation making an attempted assassination federal crime.

1968   Congress authorized the protection of widow and minor children of a former president. Due to Robert Kennedy's assassination Congress authorized protection of major presidential and vice presidential candidates and nominees.

1970   The White House Police becomes the Executive

Protection Service and is expanded to protect diplomatic missions in Washington, DC.

1971 The Secret Service begins protecting visiting heads of a foreign state or government as directed by the president.

1972, May 15 Assassination attempt on presidential candidate George Wallace, who is seriously wounded.

1974 Congress authorizes the protection of the immediate family of the vice president.

1975, September 5 Assassination attempt on President Gerald Ford by Lynette "Squeaky" Fromme in Sacramento, California.

1975, September 22 Assassination attempt on President Gerald Ford by Sara Jane Moore in San Francisco, California.

1977 The Executive Protection Service becomes the Secret Service Uniformed Division.

1981, March 30 Assassination attempt on President Ronald Reagan, who is seriously wounded.

1995, April 19 Oklahoma City field office is destroyed in the bombing of the Murrah Federal Office Building. Six agents are killed.

1998 Telemarketing Fraud Prevention Act and Identity Theft and Assumption Deterrence Act added to Secret Service responsibilities.

1999 Secret Service Memorial Headquarters Building is dedicated in Washington, DC. First building solely for the United States Secret Service.

2001, September 11 New York City field office in World Trade Center Building 7 is destroyed in the 9/11 attacks. One agent dies in rescue.

2003 United States Secret Service is transferred from the Department of the Treasury to Department of Homeland Security.

2009 First Overseas Electronic Crimes Task Force is formed.

★

Acknowledgments

For Marc and Jaime at St. Martin's Press for their inspiration and guidance in suggesting this work. And for Charles, who taught me about writing for young adults.